POLITICS IN ACTION

POLITICS

How

IN ACTION

to Make Change Happen

WILLIAM MUEHL

ASSOCIATION PRESS
NEW YORK

International Standard Book Number: 0-8096-1847-8
Library of Congress Catalog Card Number: 72-4054

Library of Congress Cataloging in Publication Data

Muehl, William.
    Politics in action.

    1. Politics, Practical. 2. Electioneering—United States. I. Title.
JK1976.M8   329'.00973   72-4054
ISBN 0-8096-1847-8

*To my colleagues
on the New Haven, Conn.,
Board of Aldermen,
1963–69*

To the Reader

The material in this book reflects over thirty years of study and experience in the field of politics. Many of its illustrations arise from my own participation in several different party organizations in four states and in a number of cities and towns. On the other hand, much of what follows has been gathered from discussions with friends who have been active politically in various parts of the country and from the numerous books and articles that I have read on the subject. Thus, it would be wholly inaccurate and unfair to try to correlate specific material contained herein with the party and personalities with which I am currently associated.

W.M.

Contents

Contents

1

The Attack on Democratic Politics

In the midst of the outbursts of violence on university campuses a distinguished psychologist interpreted youthful extremism in the following way: Our young people have tried everything else. They have written letters to Congress, petitioned the President, organized teach-ins on critical national issues, marched on Washington, and even picketed the White House. Nothing has worked. The war in Viet Nam continues; black men and women are denied full citizenship; industry persists in its massive pollution of our environment; and inexcusable poverty mocks the affluent society. The traditional methods of producing change have failed completely. So students have been driven to take violent action.

This point of view is fairly common among thoughtful people in the United States today. Even those who deplore the tactics of social disruption are often willing to explain them in terms of what they call the "failure" of democratic politics. It is widely assumed and earnestly argued that youthful intellectuals and deprived minorities have turned to violence only after exhausting the electoral remedies available to them—that democracy has been given a fair trial and found guilty of gross incompetence.

Such a reaction to the frustrations of living in a complex society is not surprising. One would need to be callously insensitive to feel no outrage in the face of war, racism, poverty, and pollution. From one perspective, vigorous social protest is both a hopeful sign and a tribute to the potential for radical self-criticism in our society. It is far healthier to have students rioting over foreign policy than over football. And even the self-destructive violence of some forms of black protest should be preferred to the racial quiescence of an earlier day.

But the demand for revolution on the ground that "traditional methods of producing change have failed completely" is based upon at least two fallacies. And these need to be examined briefly at the beginning of this discussion of grass-roots political responsibility.

First, it is a gross misreading of recent history to argue that large numbers of people—young and old, black and white, rich and poor—have tried intelligently and persistently to use the mechanism of politics in the United States to effect significant social change. The fact is that few Americans of any station in life have ever taken the trouble to understand and use our political machinery. We go through the motions of appearing to do so and speak bitterly to one another about the power of "bosses," "machines," and "the Establishment" when our purely symbolic activities fail to achieve their stated purpose. But the imaginative and sustained acceptance of political responsibility is as rare as an excess of charity. The only difference between youth and age at this point is in the vocabulary of self-exculpation. Fathers damn the politicians over coffee and cigars at service-club luncheons, while their sons denounce the system from the steps of the college library. Few of either group have ever engaged in practical politics.

Notice that the psychologist quoted above seems to feel that one has both used and exhausted "the traditional methods of producing change" when one has fired off a few petitions, marched on Washington and picketed the White House. In his misapprehension he speaks for many other critics of democracy and reveals a shocking ignorance of democracy's mode of operation. Demonstrations and other forms of direct confrontation have their place in the over-all pattern of political action. But they play at best an auxiliary role. The primary means of influencing public policy in a democracy is the election process—the business of selecting the men and program by which the nation is to be governed. Those who sway nominations and elections are the people who exercise the greatest power in democratic politics. Thus, the man who wishes to share in decision-making must be prepared to accept the responsibilities from which the power flows.

Unfortunately these responsibilities are seldom dramatic in nature. They rarely involve speech-making, the writing of foreign policy position papers, or even torchlight parades. It is easy to get a false impression of the whole process from the mass media, because in their very nature they concentrate on national politics and tend to emphasize its most exciting aspects. But even in a Presidential campaign every vivid moment in front of a television camera or before a phalanx of cheering supporters represents countless hours of deadly routine and would be impossible without them.

Thus, even among those who recognize intellectually the importance of electoral politics, there is a notable reluctance to take up the burden which this implies. And that reluctance explains a great deal of the current cynicism about traditional forms of political action. Men and women unwilling to give time to the routine tasks which add up to policy-making are often equally unwilling to confess the real reason for their reluctance. It is embarrassing to admit that one prefers a bridge game to a party caucus, that the thrill of haranguing fellow students in Old Main auditorium leaves one with little desire for addressing envelopes, or that long sessions on the town sewer budget are too high a price to pay for some small voice on larger matters. And because such admissions are hard to make we frequently substitute seemingly good reasons for real ones and declare with a despairing sigh that nothing is to be achieved through traditional political techniques. In this manner do we make virtues of our faults.

The net result of all this is that real power drifts into the hands of a relatively small proportion of the population, while the rest of us mutter angrily about conspiracy, machines, and the Establishment in order to cover our own retreat. But now let's look at a few examples showing various aspects of this problem. They may help us to see ourselves more clearly.

A few years ago when the mayor of an Eastern city was running for re-election, he was approached at a reception given in his honor by a well-known member of a college faculty, a man whose name appears frequently on the letterheads of organizations dedicated to social and political reform. The professor shook the candidate's hand vigorously, expressed deep appreciation for his fine record of constructive service, and assured him of his enthusiastic backing. The mayor thanked his well-wisher and added, "Be sure to get all your friends out next Tuesday."

A look of bewilderment came over the professor's face. "Tuesday? What's happening on Tuesday?"

With strained patience the mayor explained that there would be a municipal election on Tuesday and that his own position was at stake. He asked, "Haven't you seen stories about the campaign in the newspapers?"

"Oh," the faculty member responded disdainfully, "I

never read the local press. Just the New York *Times*."

On another occasion in a different city the militant leader of an anti-poverty crusade was urging his audience to take to the streets in revolutionary protest against slum housing.

"We have tried to work through peaceful political channels," he cried, "and have gotten nowhere. We have no alternative left but a show of force."

A newspaper reporter present began to ask some questions about the alleged unsuccessful efforts to work through "peaceful political channels." What officials had been approached and by whom? Had any responsible department refused to act upon substantial evidence of wrongdoing? Were efforts to exert pressure upon party leaders unavailing? It soon became embarrassingly clear that no real attempt had been made to use the legal remedies available in such situations. And the articulate apostle of revolution was finally reduced to the admission that he had been "speaking figuratively" in his charge that such avenues had been exhausted with no results.

The reduction to absurdity of all this occurred on the campus of a small Western college. In an effort to make itself more responsive to student concerns the faculty voted to put two undergraduates on every administrative committee and invite student participation at all faculty meetings. When this decision was announced, the president of the college was visited by an angry student-body representative. The students, it appeared, had planned a confrontation on that very issue later in the spring and were indignant at the elimination of their major grievance!

One final illustration: The emergence of a creative black self-consciousness is surely one of the most significant social phenomena of our time. The pincers of moderate reform and militant separatism have produced dramatic results for blacks in the United States whose benefits are only beginning to be felt. But in spite of much persuasive evidence of rising expectations it remains difficult to get black men and women to register, vote, and take part in the day-to-day operation of the political process, even in those Northern cities where such participation involves no personal risk for those engaged in it. Excellent black candidates have been forced to rely upon the support of white liberals because of the residual political inertia of the black community. And yet one hears it said repeatedly that our political system has failed the black citizen.

These illustrations could be multiplied many times from my own experience. And as I go around the country speaking on this general subject every audience produces two or three people who rise to report on their own encounters with the same phenomenon. It is quite clear that masses of Americans grossly misrepresent the extent of their efforts to influence the shape of the community through the process of electoral politics. They seem willing to endanger the future of democracy in order to conceal, even from themselves, the degree of their default as citizens.

Now let me make it clear that I can understand these instances of political irresponsibility. It *is* difficult for the scholar or student to make himself take sewer assessments seriously when there is engrossing work waiting on his own desk. It is tempting to try to circumvent the often slow processes of legal redress of grievances by indulging in the rewarding rhetoric of confrontation. And the long history of black oppression goes far to explain the reluctance of modern black men to become involved in the institutions which have so often been the means of their exploitation. But, while such considerations explain *why* people do not make better use of the mechanism of self-government, they are not in themselves indictments of that machinery or proof that it has failed. There may be any number of valid reasons why a man cannot learn to play the piano, but they do not serve to persuade reasonable people that the piano is an impossible or useless instrument.

It is difficult to believe that young people and minority groups are being driven to violence by the failure of democratic political procedures when one studies the distressing record of popular nonparticipation in politics. It is even more difficult to believe in light of the dramatic accomplishments of those determined people who *have* set about using effectively the neglected remedies of democracy.

A most obvious instance here, of course, is the amazing success of Senator Eugene McCarthy's effort to unseat President Lyndon Johnson in the 1968 Presidential election. Judged by any fair criteria that campaign *was* successful. It forced an incumbent President to forswear a second full term in office, drove the two major political parties to soften their previous positions on Viet Nam, and provided both the dynamic and the foundation for an aggressively effective reform movement within the national Democratic Party. It becomes increasingly clear with the passage of time that these were Senator McCarthy's real objectives and that they were attained more fully than he had ever expected.

It is important to remember that the McCarthy campaign was a political movement well within the structure of our traditional electoral process. Subsequent violent events such as the assassination of Senator Robert Kennedy and the rioting in Chicago tend to exert a kind of retrospective psychological influence and suggest that the McCarthy movement was actually cast in the mold of confrontation politics. A careful review of the facts, however, makes it obvious that the essence of that campaign is to be discerned in the New Hampshire primary, when hundreds of volunteers canvassed that state with an enthusiasm which made up in determination for what it lacked in professional gloss.

The students who went "clean for Gene" by shearing and shaving, the housewives who walked from door to door leading or carrying small children, and the other citizens who performed the McCarthy miracle were acting within the best tradition of American politics, and no subsequent violence should be allowed to distort what they proved about the viability of responsible political action.

The McCarthy movement was, however, only a large-scale version of what has been accomplished again and again at the state and local level by intelligent people willing to devote as much time to acting as they do to complaining. Three young lawyers turned the Republican Party in their Midwestern town from a standing joke into a viable and threatening competitor by organizing neighborhood discussion groups. Two students nearly toppled an entrenched machine in their college town by interviewing selected voters about their views on local government. (They did it as an honors project in political science!) A Reform Democratic group challenged one of the most successful Regular Democratic organizations on the East Coast, defeated it in a primary, and sent their own delegates to the state convention in 1968. A reading of that classic in its field, Lincoln Steffens' *Shame of the Cities,* will yield numerous examples of the overthrow of an urban boss by a group of determined amateurs.

The list of such achievements is a long one. But it will not impress those who do not want to believe in the possibility of effective democratic politics. When indifference, impatience, or the desire for ego-inflating confrontation makes men unwilling to work through the process of electoral democracy, they can always find an excuse for refusing to do so in spite of the weight of evidence against them.

The second fallacy underlying much current cynicism

about the viability of democratic politics is the failure to distinguish between procedural efficiency and substantive success. Or, to put it in simple words, the assumption that if democracy is working as it should, *my* side will win.

Here, again, there is much to be learned from the McCarthy movement of 1968. When that impressive effort failed to secure the nomination of Senator Eugene McCarthy by the Democratic National Convention at Chicago many of its most enthusiastic workers concluded bitterly that the campaign had proven the uselessness of traditional political processes. "We worked our heads off," they argued, "and McCarthy was passed over for Hubert Humphrey. Doesn't that demonstrate the corruption and futility of party politics?"

What such arguments overlook is the fact that most of the registered Democrats in the United States preferred Humphrey to McCarthy. This was made quite clear in a series of public opinion polls taken during the winter of 1967-68 and spring of 1968. Such a preference *may* have been politically wrong. It *may* have revealed an ethical obtuseness in Democrats. But it cannot be called a failure or betrayal of democracy. It can hardly be cast up as a sign of the corruption of our political system that the final outcome of the nominating convention corresponded to what the majority of registered Democrats wanted. Whatever else it may be called, that result was a vindication of the *representative* character of our institutions. It is the function of democracy to assure majority rule, not government by a passionate elite, no matter how moral the latter's intentions.

The same truth holds in all areas of our national life. If most of the citizens of a given community favor low taxes and poor schools, balanced budgets and substandard welfare payments, one cannot fairly blame the electoral process if men who advocate such policies are put into office.

And yet it is just such sad social phenomena which constitute the gravamen of many of the most vicious assaults upon our political institutions.

Any man has a right to oppose majority rule as the basis for social decision-making and many distinguished philosophers have done just that. Perhaps such elitists are right and we should be ruled by a select junta of some sort. But it is erroneous, if not dishonest, to profess to believe in democracy and then condemn the mechanism which produces democratic results because these results outrage one's personal standards.

There is, of course, a significant relationship between procedural and substantive issues in political discussion. The rules governing the operation of a local political party may be so cast as to give a consistent advantage to those who hold a particular view about important current problems. And when large numbers of citizens are denied the ballot because of their race or economic condition the line between procedure and substance gets badly blurred. In such situations it may be necessary to work outside the electoral procedure for a time, to use confrontation-type pressures in order to rectify abuses of the democratic process.

Such conditions are far less numerous, however, than the mythology of the New Left suggests. And they do not provide an ethical rationale for the cynical recourse to violence which has become too common in America. Moreover, the appropriate function of confrontation in such situations is to provide a remedy for a defect in the electoral process and not to use that defect as an excuse for making social disruption the normal mode of political expression. Street demonstrations, sit-ins, and even riots may be necessary in order to secure adherence to the principles of representative government. But a great deal is lost when the apostles of such tactics forget their original purpose and try to make violence normative.

It is tragically naïve to suppose that people who cannot be persuaded to engage in the relatively safe and simple politics of peaceful change will be able to understand and control the destructive energies unleashed by a revolution. Only a hopeless romantic can imagine that men and women who refuse to be bothered with attending party caucuses, organizing precinct committees, and getting out the vote will be able to build a bright new world on the smoking ruins of democracy. Most of the revolutions in history have produced tyrannies worse than those they have overthrown, because the complex business of starting a society from scratch requires a kind of arbitrary use of power wholly inconsistent with freedom. However serious the difficulties involved in making democratic politics work, they are minor compared to the problem of preserving humane values in the ethos of revolution.

There is dramatic testimony to the truth of this contention in an article in the New York *Times* of May 15, 1970. In this article one of the more militant leaders of the New Left was quoted as saying that his group intended to make itself "trustee" for the masses of the world and would do so even if some form of fascism were necessary in order to accomplish that end.

It seems clear, then, that one of the major responsibilities facing ethically sensitive men and women in our time is to master the procedures of democratic politics. College students have in recent months shown increasing disenchantment with the technique of confrontation as a primary mode of social protest. Large delegations of students visited Washington during the month of May 1970, and made orderly visits to the offices of their home-state legislators. They went into their interviews well prepared with facts, stated their case with courtesy, and generally made a favorable impression on the Senators and Congressmen with whom they talked. The chief foreign policy advisor to one Senator summed up the feeling of Washington officials when he said, "You just can't *help* being influenced by this kind of sustained and responsible political pressure, because you know that these people mean to stay in politics and you will have them to reckon with very shortly."

Enthusiasm and determination are, however, only short-term substitutes for political skill and sophistication. They erode quickly under the impact of repeated frustration and defeat. Even the best of intentions need to be accompanied by a working knowledge of the machinery of politics, if they are to endure and succeed.

2

The Nature of Political Parties

When Adolph Hitler launched his infamous blitzkrieg against France and the Low Countries in 1940 his armored divisions included many ordinary automobiles disguised with light wooden superstructures to look like tanks. This device led to panicky rumors that the German Army possessed an incredible number of very fast and highly maneuverable armored vehicles. The idea was Hitler's personal brainchild, scoffed at by his generals, and born of his shrewd political instinct. It proved remarkably successful and demonstrated one of the primary principles of politics: The *appearance* of power generates power and can often even substitute for it.

American politicians have known this for a long time. The political party in the United States is a product of their knowledge. Like the fearful-looking beetle whose massive shell is propelled by a fragile bug, our parties thrive on the illusion of invulnerability. Behind the façade there is far less strength, sophistication, and activity than the observer supposes, along with, at times, an almost pathetic vulnerability. The best friend of politics-as-usual in the worst sense is the eloquent cynic who proclaims the entrenched strength of party organization. For, in so do-

21

ing, he helps to create the very "fact" which he decries.
And the greatest threat to established political leadership
is not the prophet who summons men to a holy crusade
against overwhelming odds, but that simple visionary who
says quite firmly, "Why, he isn't wearing any clothes at
all!" And then proceeds to act in that confidence.

The largely psychological character of political power is
well demonstrated in the experience of a colleague of mine
on the Yale faculty. He reports:

One day, a student came to me in great distress. He had
run through a stoplight and had been arrested for reckless
driving. There was a special police crusade going on and he
had been ordered into court to stand trial. He wondered if I
knew a good lawyer who might handle his case for a reasonable fee.

I cast about in my mind and ran my eye down the column
of attorneys in the phone book. One name leaped out at me.
He was a chap my wife and I had dined with only a few weeks
before at the home of a mutual friend. I put in a call and soon
we were chatting cordially. When he heard the problem that I
put before him, he replied with hearty assurance that I was to
give it no further thought, that he would take care of everything.

The next day my student came in with relief shining in his
face and told me that the indictment had been quashed, thrown
out of court. My lawyer friend had visited the prosecutor and
had had the matter dropped. This, of course, took me completely by surprise. I had hoped merely that the attorney would
handle the case in the usual manner, but would, however,
moderate his fees in view of the student's financial condition.
What had produced this dramatic denouement?

A bit of inquiry brought out the facts. The lawyer I had
called was also, unknown to me, the majority leader in the
Town Council. The public prosecutor was of the same party
and faction. My perfectly innocent call had been interpreted
as an effort to get this boy "off the hook" by securing the

quashing of the indictment against him. And that's what had happened.

Why had the majority leader of the Town Council done this for me? Because he had assumed that only a person with substantial political influence would have dared to ask the favor which he *thought* I was asking!

But this comedy of errors was only beginning. People heard of this episode and from time to time in the next few months I was approached by persons who supposed that I had political pull. I was in the way of becoming a kind of boss!

Then, to cap the climax, my wife informed me that we had not actually dined with this particular lawyer at all; in fact, we had never met him. I had confused his name with that of another attorney.

This is, of course, an unusually dramatic manifestation of the psychological quality of much political power. My friend had phoned to ask one thing. The lawyer at the other end of the wire assumed that he was asking another and inferred that my friend must have some basis for requesting such a favor. And thus the wheels of influence were set in motion by a double case of mistaken identity.

Political power is to a considerable extent based upon just such an illusion of influence. If people *believe* that Mr. A has pull with city official B, they begin to defer to him. And seeing people defer to Mr. A, city official B often begins to grant Mr. A certain special privileges, which Mr. A then parlays into further influence with his friends and neighbors. And a circle of political inferences begins to spiral into actual power.

It should be made quite clear that the creation of such erroneous assumptions is rarely left to chance. It does not often happen accidentally, as it did to my colleague. Wherever two or three politicians come together there begins an elaborate, if informal, ritual by which each member of the group seeks to impress the others with his solid bargaining position. And one could almost keep a scorecard on the results. To be recognized and called by name by a United States Senator at a clambake is worth so many points. To be summoned aside by the Senator and engaged earnestly in solemn consultation multiplies the winnings by ten!

This basic political fact is recognized by men and women who operate at even the humblest levels of party activity. When I first entered elective politics I was overawed by the seemingly constant round of important, confidential conversations in which my colleagues engaged. Meetings of the Board of Aldermen, for example, would be delayed for a considerable period of time while pairs and trios stood at discreet distances from one another and talked intensely. What fascinating machinations were afoot I could only imagine. I longed for the day when I would be privy to such discussions.

Well, I soon learned that most of these conferences concerned sporting events, lodge outings, and family matters. Only a few had anything to do with the substance of politics. But so deeply ingrained is the politician's instinct for creating the illusion of significance that most interpersonal encounters take on the appearance of high policy consultations.

As election time approaches, the rituals of political action begin to intensify, but even in the hectic days leading up to the crucial balloting there is far less going on than one would suppose from listening to reports at Town Committee meetings. In fact, when a newcomer to the game, impressed by its linguistics, undertakes to work as energetically as the veterans talk he is likely to be regarded as a prodigy, a dangerous fanatic, or a combination of the two. There are few areas of life in which illusion plays as important a part as it does in politics.

It would be a mistake, however, to conclude from all

this that political parties in the United States are relatively weak and disintegrated because politicians are dishonest scamps who care more for deception than responsibility. Such an analysis sets the proverbial cart before the horse. It is not the disposition of politicians but the infirmity of our institutions which puts a premium upon the manipulation of illusion. The politician who creates the appearances of power is often as not responding to the absence of a responsible power base in his constituency. He is the victim of political paralysis, not its perpetrator. And many of the rituals in which he engages are the liturgies by which some degree of stability and consensus is created under most difficult circumstances.

There is no space here for a full discussion of the historical factors which have made political disintegration so characteristic of life in the United States. But there are a few things which must be said in order to lay a foundation for what is to come.

Americans are *in theory* an intensely individualistic people who deeply distrust political solutions to the problems of the community. The men and women who settled the New World and established its traditions were in a state of rebellion against various forms of social institutions in the nations from which they had fled. They were dissenters in religious, economic, social, and political terms. And they had learned to equate politics with government, and government with tyranny. Their worst suspicions in this respect were quickly confirmed by New England theocracies and royal governors. Very soon the open-ended atmosphere of this sprawling continent led to rebellion against political power, not simply in the organized American Revolution but in a cultural spasm which rejected authority of every kind and put a high premium on all forms of voluntarism.

The world and the nation have changed radically since

the days of Thomas Jefferson. But the mythology of our anti-political tradition still thrives in the hearts of most Americans. People who live on Social Security, demand larger Medicare benefits, and insist upon the need for more "law and order" are among the most vociferous in their denunciations of "big government" and "conniving politicians." This paradox was incarnate in the late Dwight D. Eisenhower who in all of his adult life enjoyed the total security benefits of his Army status and yet persistently condemned the welfare state. And it can be seen in those young people today who demand what are essentially political solutions to pressing social problems, while fulminating against Washington "bureaucrats."

This pathological fear of government power has played the major role in forming the American political party, for the tendency to equate politics with potential tyranny has inhibited the evolution of responsible and effective party organization at every level of our national life. And it is this false equation of responsible political processes with tyrannical government which now poses one of the most serious threats to our freedom. For nothing is more likely to bring on authoritarianism than a rapidly proliferating demand for government services without a correlative development of effective political action.

Perhaps the most immediate and dramatic impact of our anti-government bias upon political parties is to be seen in the American tradition of part-time politics. It is one of the major tenets of our national creed that our political leaders must appear to be amateurs, that their primary *raison d'etre* lie outside the realm of politics, and that they must long for nothing so much as an opportunity to lay aside the cares of state and return to farming or to the practice of law in some small town.

This Cincinnatus-and-the-plow psychology may strike one as nothing more serious than superficial romanticism.

But it is the basis for many of the most significant infirmities of our political system. For it drives some of the more important party functions underground, compels us to transact a great deal of political business in a nonpolitical context, and thus prevents the general public from participating in crucial decision-making processes.

In most American communities, for example, the two major political parties maintain no official headquarters, have no professional staff workers between election campaigns, and hold no meetings of their governing bodies until it is time for the nominating process to begin. In short, politics is laid away in mothballs except for brief periods surrounding elections. This fits in nicely with the accepted picture of the good politician as a purely part-time public servant. Any attempt to deviate from the customary pattern and establish some kind of organizational continuity or party headquarters between elections is likely to be interpreted as a subtle power play or an effort to make a job for someone's sister-in-law.

As a result of this insistence upon informality and fear of structure there are few occasions upon which party members have an opportunity to discuss even the most important matters of political policy. The myth that politics is unimportant and need not be institutionalized responsibly means that issues are debated and conclusions reached wherever political figures happen to come together for more legitimate purposes. If the leaders of a party belong to the same country club, lodge, or church, decisions vitally affecting thousands of people will be made casually over a putter or a cup of coffee. In almost every city and town there are certain restaurants in which the political elite gathers several times a week for lunch. And it is often possible for the acute observer to make accurate predictions about the shape of things to come by noting who is eating with whom.

Thus, it is often literally true that the accident of one man's presence at the table on a crucial day may be the decisive factor in the formulation of some significant governmental policy. There is no planned agenda for such sessions, and no invitations are extended to interested parties. Those who turn up, whether deliberately or by coincidence, are the ones upon whose shoulders the mantle of power falls. It is not at all uncommon, for example, for a member of some legislative body to go to one of its sessions expecting full deliberation on a piece of legislation only to discover that a group of his influential colleagues happened to attend a social event the night before and settled the issue for all practical purposes.

This kind of experience easily leads to a conspiracy theory of politics. The assumption is that the decision-makers have deliberately met behind closed doors in order to foil the democratic process. Sometimes, of course, this is the case. But more often, in my experience, the villain is not the demonic intentions of wicked men, but the absence from our political process of those formal, planned occasions on which specified matters can be taken up and all interested persons given an opportunity to be heard. Decisions are made casually because Americans insist upon perpetuating the notion that politics is something to be done with the left hand on an occasional free weekend.

In immediate terms the most exasperating result of this procedure is the drift of power into the hands of those who happen to be on hand when decisions are to be made. But in the long run the more serious result is the fragmentation which this style of politics imposes upon government and the manner in which it frustrates honest efforts to use political parties as vehicles for the advancement of coherent and consistent social policy.

It will be difficult for any political novice to understand the perpetuation of this state of affairs until he takes seriously the significance of our part-time politics and its impact upon the operation of the democratic process in America. So let us examine briefly the mechanics of party operation.

The Machine

When men come together to form political parties and work for the election of some of their number to public office, their activities inevitably generate power. By their ability to grant or withhold nominations, to give financial support to some candidates and stint others, and their legal status as agencies of the electoral process, parties are able to exact a degree of respect and even obedience from candidates and officeholders.

Theoretically the power which this process generates is dispersed throughout the whole organization in reasonably democratic fashion. And at critical times, most notably on the eve of elections, the theory is followed in practice. Delegates from the various geographic areas represented within the district come together to draw up a platform, choose candidates, and name party leadership for the next stipulated legal interval.

In those democracies in which there is a strong tradition of full-time political organization, the handling of party power tends to be reasonably democratic, even between campaigns. That is to say, there are established channels of communication and control through which the membership is kept in touch with headquarters and headquarters is made aware of sentiment in the hustings. In England, for example, party conferences are held from time to time for the express purpose of giving voice to membership opinion and opportunity for leaders to interpret problems and policies. In various forms the same general procedure takes place in other democratic nations.

In the United States, however, our tradition of part-time amateur politics, along with our tendency to deny the important role of party organization, has made it difficult to establish patterns of democratic control within the major parties. By refusing to accept the necessity for party activity between elections we have complicated legitimate efforts to distribute power throughout the structure of political organizations.

This fact was brought home to me with dramatic impact very early in my own political career during a critical gubernatorial election campaign. In the days leading up to the actual balloting I worked closely with party leaders in my small hometown. They had managed to achieve a reasonable degree of efficiency in their activities. We made voter lists, lined up rides for people who needed them, arranged for baby-sitters, and did all the things that constitute traditional electioneering. The office from which we worked was well staffed and equipped. Files were in order and area maps kept up to the minute on new registrations. A visitor would have been impressed by the appearance of competence and enthusiasm.

On Election Day itself an amazing thing happened. Steadily, from dawn to dusk, the order and efficiency of that headquarters deteriorated. Cards on voters were thrown in careless heaps on tables instead of being returned to alphabetized files. Records of every kind were scattered about the room in random fashion. Maps were torn apart and given to drivers for use in locating particular neighborhoods. Every imaginable violation of sound organizational procedure was repeated over and over.

We won the election. The next day janitors came into the erstwhile party headquarters, swept up most of those carefully compiled records, and burned them. The following year that local organization had to spend weeks reassembling its basic materials.

This is admittedly an extreme example. But it reflects the strong hold that election-centered psychology has on our American political parties. When I subsequently suggested to some of the workers that this seemed to be a shortsighted and wasteful way to operate, their reply was to ask what good that stuff was after the votes had been counted. Reference to the fact that there would be another election in two years was met with the kind of look given to people who talk about the end of the world! None of the election volunteers in that headquarters had any real stake in sustained party efficiency.

The result of this psychology has been to *force,* and I use that word advisedly, a great deal of power into the hands of the men who *do* have a stake in party continuity and who are in a position to accept the authority that the rank and file cast aside. (This might almost be a definition of an American political *machine.*)

When the election is over, when the volunteers have returned to their other interests, when there is no money coming in with which to pay for a meeting hall, and with the crusaders of yesterday being depicted in the press as swine with their snouts in the public trough, the mechanism by which parties are supposed to be run disintegrates rapidly. But the job that the party is required to do continues to need doing. Some effort must be made to coordinate legislators' positions on future issues. Trends in public opinion must be studied and their implications projected. The performance of those elected to public office has to be watched and their qualification for advancement analyzed. Myriad details of integrating and correlating data have to be handled.

The chief source of the power of political machines, then, is the default of democratic mechanisms *within* the party. It is neither the natural corruption of politicians nor the failure of voters to attend to their responsibilities at election time. It is the complete collapse of membership participation in party responsibility between campaigns. Political machines, like any human enterprise, are subject to fearful abuses. They are more open to corruption than many other aggregations of power, because they have developed in response to the abdication of power by those who ought to be handling it. The fact that they operate under cover as a concession to the American anti-political bias makes opportunities for abuse particularly difficult to resist and prevent. But, far from being inherently the fiendish contrivances of wicked men, they are the inevitable by-products of the efforts of our political individualism to ignore the complex realities of social process.

It is often difficult to see the full truth of this last allegation because of the publicity given to those very dramatic situations in which machine rule maintains itself by methods quite unrelated to the source of its original power. In some urban areas the dominant political organizations engage in every conceivable form of skulduggery. They intimidate voters, stuff ballot boxes, vote the cemeteries, and so on. But these situations are not typical. Taking the country as a whole they are not even common. It is the emphasis put upon them by the mass media which leads people to regard them as classical models of the political machine in operation. In the overwhelming number of American communities, urban and rural, the political machine is nothing more sinister than that which fills the vacuum left by the failure of other citizens to carry their full responsibility in the realm of politics.

There is, however, another reason for the perpetuation of the machine which needs to be mentioned here. Perhaps the best way to state it is to describe an incident reported many years ago by Lincoln Steffens.

A social worker was talking one day with a political

boss about the problems of depressed people in urban areas. She knew that scores of men and women in her own city went to representatives of the political machine whenever they were in trouble. This the social worker found hard to understand. After all, she reasoned, there are many agencies whose sole aim is to furnish aid in such situations. When she expressed this sentiment to the boss, he laughed scornfully.

"Sure," he said in effect, "when a man goes to a social agency they see to it that he gets justice. But he doesn't want *justice*. He wants help!"

This is a great source of strength for a political machine. In a government of laws it stands between the individual case and the inexorable workings of justice. Because we have created a government of laws, we have created what might be called a flexibility vacuum, the need for some "give." When a young Puerto Rican gets in trouble in New York City or an old settler in California needs help with the property laws, there is generally someone ready to pick up a telephone and speak a mediating word to the man or agency at the other end of the wire. And since that wire runs two ways, he can be sure that the phone will ring some day and that it will be his turn to perform.

Even if there were no other basis for machine organization in politics, and the parties functioned with perfect and democratic effectiveness in all respects, there would still be established within the framework of laws little networks of letters and telephone calls traced by the need of all government for an element of human flexibility.

A political machine, then, is a structure of informal relationships by which the integrating and coordinating functions of a political party are carried on in the face of electoral default and by which the rigid requirements of justice are modified in the name of humanity. Political machines *can* become the vehicles of incredible corruption; and they often do. They are inadequate responses to a substantial need, an undercover means of doing what ought to be done in properly established and supervised ways. *This* is the source of their degradation, and not the quality of their leaders or the nature of their basic functions.

The Boss

Just as the machine is in the eyes of most Americans the source of political corruption, so "the boss" is thought of as the evil genius who pilots the machine. There is certainly a great deal of evidence to support this view. Whenever one thinks of political chicanery the names of the most infamous political bosses in history come quickly to mind. And the biography of corruption in many of our large cities could apparently be written in terms of the acts and ambitions of one or two key political figures. It is no wonder that the boss lurks in the shadows of the political scene wafting to the audience the distinct smell of brimstone.

If we turn from the spectacular and atypical situations, however, and study the workings of political leadership in the average town or rural area, the demonism theory of political bossism becomes untenable. More often than not, the source of a boss's power lies in the willingness of his friends, neighbors, and associates to lay their civic responsibilities on his shoulders. Here, for example, is a fairly typical "boss biography" in my own paraphrase of the words in which it was told to me:

I was the only one in my neighborhood organization who had a typewriter . . . and I knew how to run a mimeograph machine. The boys began pushing the clerical work off on me, and I did it because no one else seemed willing. I sat up late at night writing letters, getting out handbills, and compiling lists of every kind imaginable. It was dull work. But I found that it was a great way to learn everything there is to know about a party. I memorized the dates and forms for filing petitions and submitting financial reports to the state. I learned to know what party members would pitch in and help with time and money—and what ones wouldn't. People who needed information got to calling me up for it. My name and phone number came to be identified in a lot of people's minds with the party.

Well, the next thing I knew people were asking me to speak a word for them to So-and-So at city hall or even at the statehouse. At first I felt pretty backward about doing it. But soon I found that all those letters going out over my name had made the name mean something. At least it looked familiar to the boys at the capital. And before long I had a reputation for being able to get things done. Not big things, you understand, but tickets for the governor's ball, reservations at crowded hotels, World Series passes, and stuff like that. Well, the more of this I did, the more contacts I made and the more people felt obligated to me. So every year the things I could do got a little more important. And the things I was asked to do did the same. Now they tell me I'm one of the big shots in the state. And I guess I am.

This is, of course, an abbreviated paraphrase of an oversimplified (and probably somewhat laundered) account. But it states the central truth about boss power. What my informant did not say was that he had learned in time how to write up reports of local happenings in such a way as to reflect credit and discredit on the right people, how he became friendly with a couple of newspapermen and in return for little favors and inside tips was able to shape their treatment of his friends and faction, and how he managed to remind some party notables of important legal and social events while "forgetting" to notify others.

These omitted details do not alter the picture significantly. His strength still lay in the fact that he alone had accepted responsibilities which others could have shared, and this brought him a great deal of power. It is interesting to note that to this day the boss of whom I am speaking is still doing a great deal of his party's clerical work himself. He has learned how to garner influence *and how to keep it!*

It is not unusual for a politician to become a boss without fully realizing that it is happening. Several influential men have assured me, with no reason to lie, that they did not know how significant a role they had begun to play until they read in the press or heard on the radio that their vote was expected to decide some important appointment or resolve a significant conflict of opinion in the party. A prominent New England political reporter and commentator expressed the opinion that this is probably the truth. Political power is invisible and subtle. It is, therefore, hard to measure. It can begin on a very small scale and snowball to tremendous proportions in no time at all.

The primary reason for this phenomenon is, again, the indirect character of political action and leadership in the United States. A man or woman can do many of the things that are essential to the development of political power without realizing that this will be the end result of such undertakings. Chairmanship of some local charity with the publicity attendant upon such a position, an important role in one's ethnic or religious community, a keen personal interest in one aspect of government operations such as education or tax assessments—any one of these may give a man the kind of influence which leads to political muscle, and the combination of several can be a sure formula for success. A New York district leader, now deceased, ascribed his prominence to the fact that during World War II he and a politically influential neighbor were part of the same car pool. And during the Republican National Convention in 1952 one of the major kingmakers, while being interviewed on television, admitted ruefully that his "career" had begun when he spoke up angrily at a PTA meeting about conditions on the school playground.

"My neighbors," he said, "kept pushing me to do something about the matter. And the first thing I knew I was not only in politics up to my neck but had been chosen to the executive committee of my state party."

Admittedly one who accumulates power in some such way must have a basic interest in politics to begin with. My point here is not to suggest that political bosses are reluctant dragons who fall into office or succumb to forces beyond their control. It would be as naïve to suppose that as it would be to accept the prevailing view that the boss is a megalomaniac who conspires with the demonic forces in the community for control of a large bloc of votes. The gist of these last few paragraphs has been to point out that under the rules of the game in the United States political power is not always won by direct assault and may, indeed, be the result of quite subtle combinations of nonpolitical factors. Let me close this phase of the subject with a quotation from a friend who is himself something of a political power in my home community:

"Have you ever noticed how many political bigshots are bachelors or men who married late in life? That's because even going to a stranger's wake is better than returning to that lonely hall bedroom in the boardinghouse. And you meet a helluva lot of people at a good wake!"

What does the boss get out of all this? There is a tendency to answer that question in dramatic and exaggerated terms. It arises, like our understanding of machine corruption, from a preoccupation with the most infamous of the large urban situations. No doubt the leaders and lieutenants of a few big-city organizations make impressive gains from their power to dispense favors. There is no reason to ignore such an obvious fact. But, if we return once more to the typical American situation, the kind in which most of us are involved or will become involved, the answer is quite different.

Most of the political bosses in the cities and counties of the United States never receive any direct cash pay-off for the real energy that they expend in directing the affairs of their party. It is safe to say that in all but a few cases the ability of a political boss to profit from his power depends upon his being in or getting into some enterprise in which he can legally do business with the government or with those who, through him, wish to do business with the government. (In many cases a political leader gets nothing more for his pains than a flow of free publicity for his grocery store or florist shop.)

This fact of life is so generally true that one can often trace the pattern of power in an unfamiliar neighborhood by looking into a few favorite political professions. Who gets the city's insurance business, its construction contracts? Who supplies groceries to county institutions? From whose automobile agency does the state buy its cars and trucks? And so on.

In some instances the business relations of the boss with the units of government in which he is politically active cannot stand investigation. Prices are padded, quality lowered, and stocks accumulated beyond all reasonable need. But in at least as many other cases the profit-taking by political leadership is quite legal in most respects. Where sealed bids are not required, for example, the boss's firm will simply be informed of the lowest price stipulated in a competitive bid and can then shave it by a few dollars and thus qualify for the contract. At other times an excellent case can be made for retaining the firm owned by the boss because he has had so much experience in doing government work that he is actually the most efficient and economical operator to hire. This is especially likely to be true in road construction, for example.

There are many political leaders who never have any direct dealings with government agencies. They reap their harvest through those enterprises and personalities that *do* want franchises or contracts. Thus, a lawyer in politics may find that he is retained by clients who suppose that he enjoys a favored position vis-à-vis the courts. A druggist discovers that his sales increase with his political status, because people feel that it is wise to be friendly with a man of influence. A restaurant owner can make profitable use of his banquet rooms on the same principle.

However one may feel about the undesirable possibilities inherent in such relationships, they do not violate any law and are a far cry from the kind of graft that the popular imagination associates with political bosses and machines. In fact, one can make the case that they are actually nothing worse than the extension into political life of practices which are widely followed and generally approved in business.

What has been said about the workings of political bosses may strike some readers as naïve. Certainly if one sets it next to the most infamous examples of the political machine stereotype, it looks inaccurate. So I repeat that the most notorious abuses of political power are by no means typical. They represent special circumstances and create problems quite different from those with which the average politically responsible American has to deal. I have put major emphasis upon the common kind of situation both because it is more common and because the journalistic tendency to highlight the atypical and corrupt demoralizes the very people who need to be encouraged to become active in politics. Political bosses, like the political machines which they operate, serve an important purpose in a nation which does not take its political processes seri-

ously. Their strength is largely dependent upon the apathy
and ignorance of the great mass of voters. And the wonder
is not that their power is so often abused but that it is so
frequently exercised in honest and responsible fashion.

3

Sources of Political Power

Shortly before Election Day in a small New England town, a delegation from the League of Women Voters called on the Democratic candidate for the office of First Selectman. They wanted to question him about his qualifications and platform. The women, accustomed to being handled with kid gloves by most politicians, noted with surprise that this particular man was giving them a very cool reception. Finally one of their number sought to establish their claim to his attention by asking, "Do you know what the League of Women Voters is?"

"Yes," snapped the candidate. "It is a group of high-minded women who always carefully study the qualifications of both candidates and then invariably vote the straight Republican ticket."

In a subsequent conversation with a close friend of the candidate, I expressed amazement that he should be willing to alienate an influential group of voters.

"Don't worry about Dave," was the answer. "He knows just where all his votes are coming from. And those gals can't give him any or take any of them away."

This episode involved both an inaccurate assessment of the League of Women Voters and an unwarranted tribute to the Republican Party. But, nevertheless, it dramatizes one of the less recognized facts of political life in the United States.

The Controlled Vote

When the average voter thinks of political power he is likely to think of it as something stored in bulk in a vast reservoir that can be tapped at any point by a clever political leader. He listens to speeches, reads press releases, and watches the antics of campaigning on the assumption that they are intended to swing masses of votes from one party to the other. The process of winning an election seems to most of us something akin to saturation bombing. One hurls a variety of appeals broadcast in the hope of hitting as many diverse responses as possible.

The professional politician sees the whole business in a different light. Vote-getting is for him a pin-pointed operation. It is based upon the people, groups, and institutional loyalties of the community—and a thorough familiarity with the voting record of all of these. The traditional political leader believes that the outcome of an election depends not upon *how* the people vote but upon *which* people vote. He concentrates his efforts, therefore, not on trying to swing masses of unaffiliated electors into line behind his ticket, but on seeing to it that all those who can be counted upon to vote his way are registered and get into the polling places on Election Day.

Those whose orientation is toward national political campaigns may find this difficult to understand. Why does the local politician ignore the opportunity to make capital of dramatic issues and rally masses of voters to his position? There are several answers to this question:

First, the average political organization is badly under-staffed with issue-oriented talent. It may be able to enlist numerous neighborhood canvassers, men and women who know the territory and can call most of the residents by name, and are prepared to carry on the mechanical business of campaigning with relative efficiency. But at the grass-roots level neither party has access to the kind of people who feel competent to deal with complicated issues.

The newcomer to politics is likely to be dumbfounded, for example, by how little interest his most enthusiastic supporters show in his attitude toward controversial social problems. One young candidate for the state assembly went to the first meeting of his district committee prepared to read a White Paper setting forth his position on several important questions. When he announced his plan to the district chairman he was told in no uncertain terms that this was just not done.

"These folk," the chairman said, "will go out and work their tails off for you as a person. But if you get them to arguing about these 'issues' of yours, you're going to scare a lot of them off before we even get organized."

The chairman was quite typical and quite right in his appraisal of the situation. Grass-roots political workers are party and personality oriented. They do not pretend to have mastered the intricacies of fiscal and administrative policy. Unless moved by some dramatic turn of events to do otherwise, they trust the candidates who are nominated by the party to understand and deal competently with the issues which will arise during their terms of office.

It is not a slur upon either the intelligence or civic-mindedness of these loyal men and women to recognize this fact. In many cases their reluctance to engage in the discussion of issues reflects their fear of embarrassing the candidate and/or their realization that government is a far more complex affair than many of their articulate critics realize.

Whatever the reason, however, the overwhelming ma-

jority of those who make up the working cadres of our
political parties do not see the education of the electorate
on substantive matters as a part of their job. So, when an
issue-oriented candidate or faction within the party moves
toward a campaign based upon a wide-scale public debate
on policy, the number of party regulars who can shift
easily and effectively into this mode of operation is small.

Second, politicians are instinctively afraid of stirring up
the electorate in vague and undisciplined ways. They have
learned from experience that an aroused citizenry is dangerous to everyone falling under the heading "Genus Politician." They have seen an indiscreet choice of campaign
issues lead, for example, to a reform wave that swept both
major parties into the scrap heap. At times a tactless
charge or proposal has been known to bring about a search-
ing inquiry and even an investigation by a higher echelon
of government. Thus, any technique of campaigning whose
results cannot be reasonably predicted and controlled is
frowned upon by the average political leader. He is in the
business of politics and is unlikely to do anything that
will upset the market, even though it may bring him a
short-term gain. Just as an automobile dealer is not inclined to expose the real weaknesses of his competitor's
product for fear of having the same treatment meted out
to himself, so the politician will avoid trying to win an
election by tactics that may snap back in unexpected ways.
The balance of terror was a feature of American political
life long before the A-bomb introduced it into international affairs.

Third, all politicians are guided by two primary objectives. One is, of course, the winning of the election. The
other, equally important, is maintaining control of the
party organization. Here, again, issues can be a bit dan-

gerous. When you stir up public passions and encourage political participation of a general and uncontrollable kind, you expose the established machine to risk of grave challenge. People who get really excited about politics are likely to want some continuing and effective voice in political decisions at all levels. They may be dissatisfied with the program and personnel that the party is offering. They will undoubtedly expect better performance than can be extracted from existing leadership. Some of them will throw their weight behind minority factions within organizational ranks or even put up men of their own choosing for the inner councils of power.

For the professional politician, then, the most desirable basis of power is a controlled vote. Not in the sense of being able to dictate what individuals are allowed in the polls or which votes shall be counted, but in the sense of being able to motivate certain elements in the community to vote in predictable ways. This will explain a phenomenon of American politics that many people have found difficult to understand—the relative coolness of the major parties toward support of an active kind from volunteer groups. In almost every Presidential election, for example, one of the greatest headaches that the candidates have to cope with is the friction that inevitably develops between Citizens for So-and-So and the regular organization. Amateurs have a way of stimulating voter interest to an unseemly degree and this bodes ill for the quiet and orderly life that machine tenders enjoy. In many elections Republican and Democratic professionals spend as much time trying to short-circuit their own volunteers as they do fighting one another.

This has also been the fate of labor's political action movements. In some states they have been welcomed by party regulars. In many others they have been given clearly to understand that their help is not wanted. Their money is as good as anyone's; their votes the party is happy to have. But as for their nasty habit of working at the grass roots to do many of the things that the party does not want done—this had better be left to those who understand politics!

So vigorous is the opposition of some politicians to anything that threatens their hold on the party machinery that is it not unheard of for the regulars to throw an election, deliberately sabotaging their own candidates, in order to destroy fractious elements within their ranks. This happened in flagrant fashion in a Midwestern gubernatorial contest some years ago. One of the major parties had experienced the rapid rise to prominence of a man who was in no sense a party stalwart. He had earned an excellent reputation by service in the Federal Government. His following within the local organization was small but vociferous. And his name aroused such public enthusiasm that he was clearly someone to be taken seriously.

Since the impending election looked like a bad one for his party (a variety of factors presaged defeat), this distinguished man was given the nomination. But having given him the nomination the party then proceeded to give him the "treatment." Inquiries at numerous headquarters throughout the state revealed that the regular machine was doing little or nothing to elect its candidate. No cars were available for registering voters. Absentee ballots had to be pried out of the men who should have been distributing them freely. And many town and county candidates openly disavowed the head of their ticket. In short, he was made a horrible example for those who might in the future try to circumvent the established channels of advancement within the party. When he lost the election, through no fault of his own, his defeat was cited for years afterward as evidence of the incompetence of party irregulars.

Looked at from any point of view this sort of performance is inexcusable. But it makes a certain amount of sense to one who has accepted the traditional lines of authority and is accustomed to thinking in terms of the orthodox exploitation of party strength. The willingness to throw an election in order to maintain the status quo organizationally is a natural outgrowth of the personality orientation of American political life. Politicians work long and hard to build up their contacts, to familiarize themselves with the people who make up their constituency. Since most of them have little interest in abstract political principles, they come to think of their network of personal relationships and influence not as a tool of the party, but as the party itself. The focal point of party purpose becomes for them the web of interdependence in which they are involved.

Considered from this point of view, the bright-eyed young man who plunges carelessly into this carefully balanced structure of reciprocities is actually endangering the entire party structure. His disregard for seniority, precedence, and protocol, his emphasis upon issues over which the very core of the faithful may be divided—these loom as terrible threats to what seems to party leaders to be the essence of their organization.

To some extent, of course, the arguments that party regulars advance to resist any infusion of new blood are rationalizations of their own desire to retain power. But there is also good reason to suppose that they reflect a hard fact of political life. History furnishes a number of examples of parties that have soared like skyrockets under the impetus of some aggressive newcomer or Young Turk faction, only to disintegrate disastrously after the first blaze of glory. This has been paticularly true of reform movements. They often sweep down upon the established organization, seize power by something approaching acclamation, perform brilliantly for a short time, and then fall apart. They lack the intricate, durable structure of loyalty, know-how, and self-interest that holds the traditional party core together through many difficult days. The reluctance of political veterans to involve large numbers of unpredictable and undisciplined people in party governance is not wholly indefensible.

The dependence of the orthodox political mind upon a controlled vote accounts for the fact that politicians tend to be somewhat less impressed by public opinion polls than the general populace. In the historic 1948 campaign, for example, there was less defeatism about the chances of Harry Truman among professional politicians than there was among his nonprofessional supporters. Granted that very few people in either category thought that Mr. Truman had a chance for re-election, the battle-scarred veterans of ward skirmishes were less pessimistic than the average Democrat. They understood the importance of *who actually votes* and knew from experience that this factor is difficult to measure by mass polling techniques.

Perhaps we can sum up what has been said so far in this way: Political power, like other kinds of power, is not something that a leader creates upon demand by direct access to the raw material of human conviction and necessity. A large part of it is generated by the skillful movement of pieces, each of which has a recognized function and value.

Now let us look at some of the counters that are most often found where this game of politics is played.

Personal Contacts

During my second campaign for the New Haven Board of Aldermen in 1965 I was making some door-to-door visits in my ward and encountered my opponent engaged in the same process. He seemed a bit dispirited and as we talked the reason became obvious. In his calls he had been encountering registered Republicans who had told him courteously that they planned to vote for me. Why? Because they were personal friends or associated with me in some community organization or other. Since my opponent was a man of strong Republican convictions and believed wholeheartedly that men should vote on the basis of principle, this phenomenon troubled him. As well it might.

And yet nothing becomes more clear with experience in politics than the fact that large numbers of people allow their decisions in every election to be determined by their personal association with one of the candidates or his supporters. So well established is this pattern that any deviation from it is likely to be misinterpreted by politicians themselves. When you talk with an active party worker at the grass roots, for example, and tell him that you plan to support for nomination someone with whom you are only slightly acquainted, the chances are very good that he will read your decision as evidence of a personal feud between you and one or more of the other candidates for the office in question. Discussion of issues is often regarded as a cover-up for some interpersonal antagonism. I have never forgotten a conversation in which after some time spent in explaining my substantive reason for preferring Mr. A to Mr. B. and thinking that I had managed finally to make my point, the man to whom I had been speaking asked plaintively, "But what have you *really* got against Mr. B.?

This attitude reflects the average politician's realistic appraisal of the basis of his own strength and that of both his colleagues and his opponents. The strong candidate or leader is the one who enjoys a great variety of social contacts, one who will garner votes on the basis of his personal popularity.

The significance of these contacts can be seen in the frequency with which they are advanced as qualifications for nomination and even election. Time and time again when candidates for office are invited to cite their fitness for the post they are seeking, their replies consist chiefly of a long list of the fraternal, civic, and religious organizations to which they belong. The men who answer thus do not do so out of the thoughtful conviction that such associations in fact qualify them for election. Their replies merely reflect the extent to which the importance of these contacts has been drummed into them during years of party activity.

Ethnic Groups

An interested student of social patterns in the United States can learn much about population shifts in this country by studying the ballots of the two major parties over a period of twenty years. For, with few notable exceptions, the choice of candidates in local and state elections reflects the relative strength and self-consciousness of various ethnic groups within the community.

Such a student would discover, for example, that there is an increasing number of Italian-American names on city and state tickets throughout the whole Eastern half of the nation. He could trace the decline of Yankee power in New England and the rise of the Irish to positions of prominence; the gradual displacement of the Irish by the more recently arrived Italians, and the crowding of these last in the present decade by militant black Americans seeking their place in the political sun.

One of the most potent and dependable sources of political power is to be found in self-conscious minority groups in any area. This fact does not reflect simply personal associations. It springs from the discovery by struggling new Americans that one of the channels through which they can achieve dignity and an opportunity for economic advancement is politics. In the voting booth there is no measurement of traditional social acceptability. The vote of an O'Rourke or a Gambardella counts for as much as that of a Saltonstall or a Cabot. And the color of the hand that pulls the party lever does not lessen the impact of the ballot at all. By throwing their votes to the party that gives them the most desirable spots on the ticket, minority ethnic groups have managed to acquire real political influence in the life of the nation.

Thus, the ability to woo and win the various ethnic minorities with flattery and patronage is a vital element in political success everywhere in the United States. In the play, *The State of the Union,* the comment of a candidate for President that he had "always thought the Poles voted in Poland" showed inexcusable naïveté, as indeed it was intended to do.

Fear and Favor

Contemporary psychologists tell us that the strongest motivation is the hope of reward plus a moderate fear of penalty. This is a truism that politicians learn through experience and have known for a long time. It operates at three levels of sophistication:

1. Among relatively simple and uneducated people, ward and precinct leaders have often been remarkably successful in planting the idea that "the party knows how you vote." Sometimes this is explained in terms of the allegedly different sound of the bells on the voting machine, at other times by other means. But of one thing a great many unsophisticated Americans are sure. The party knows how they vote. Thus, they willingly accept the no-

tion that they will be rewarded when they vote properly and punished when they vote improperly.

There is, of course, a degree of reality to this picture. Party poll watchers can often tell by the length of time that a man spends in the voting booth whether he is voting the straight ticket or splitting his ballot. On occasion an individual's voting record can be ferreted out by conversations with indiscreet friends and neighbors. But, added all together, the number of instances in which a man's vote is not secret is small indeed.

Nevertheless, so long as people accept this myth, they will be susceptible to pressures and temptations, selling their vote for promises and threats, fixed tickets, the fear of draft reclassification, and so on. This belief is a reservoir of power occasionally tapped by unscrupulous politicians.

2. At a somewhat more sophisticated level, the use of fear and favor is equally successful and more understandably so. These are the voters who stand to gain by the party's victory and have something to lose by its defeat. Here is where the patronage element enters the scene. Government employees, their wives, parents, and friends know there is much at stake for the individual in the fate of his party. The hope of getting a job or the fear of losing one is a handy source of solidarity among both Republicans and Democrats.

It is not only among government employees that this factor operates. It can also be seen in the restaurant proprietor who wants a liquor or floor-show license, the apartment-house owner who has been allowed to ignore a fire code technicality, and the man whose road has been kept better plowed by one administration than by another! These people are under no misapprehension about the ability of party leaders to read their ballots. They simply have something at stake in the victory of one party or faction.

3. Finally, we have the top level of sophistication, those who feel in a general way that things are better for everyone when a particular party occupies city hall or the statehouse. Sometimes this represents the unconscious rationalization of a specific fear or personal ambition. At other times it arises from the honest conviction that "our kind" ought to run things.

Politicians play to this last attitude constantly. The candidate standing on the platform in his shirt sleeves is trying to persuade laborers that their fate will be better in his hands. The gentleman in a conservative necktie who is pictured with his obviously genteel wife and well-scrubbed children seeks to insinuate himself into the confidence of professional and business men. These, too, are playing to the fear-and-favor eyes of their audiences.

It is easy to wax indignant about this element in our political life. And at its most primitive level it is an abuse to be deplored. But there is something inevitable and even constructive about the candid recognition that the function of democratic institutions is to represent the real concerns of real people, and not a set of abstractions to which public officials give lip service on state occasions. If those concerns turn out to be narrowly selfish or dangerously unwise, this unfortunate fact will reflect itself in the operation of representative government.

We have seen, then, that the orthodox politician likes to think of his craft as the skillful manipulation of known quantities. He tends to shrink from any campaign tactics that might stir up the uncommitted and unpredictable elements in the electorate and would rather lose an occasional election than endanger the patterns of controlled voting

that give him dominance in his own party and avoid mu-
tually destructive interparty conflict.

Thus, the primary and often exclusive emphasis in map-
ping out pre-election strategy is known as "getting out our
vote." It is clearly an article of faith with many political
leaders that their supporters always outnumber the opposition and that the only real challenge to the organization
is to be sure that their entire constituency reaches the polls
on Election Day. No matter how heavily the tide of issues
may run against a particular organization, no matter how
inevitable its defeat may have been in the light of substantive positions on pressing problems, the standard explana-
tion the morning after a lost election is: "They got out
their vote and we didn't!" And I have heard this said
solemnly even when the statistics made the statement pat-
ently untrue.

The controlled election is obviously a perversion of the
democratic process. Candidates are chosen on the basis of
group contacts, campaigns conducted in such a way as to
conceal rather than clarify issues, and the election reveals
nothing about the public will except its weakness. Party
leadership remains in power not because of its effectiveness in formulating policy and choosing personnel, but on
the basis of its skill in playing a highly complicated game.

One need not have a great deal of experience to realize
that the politician's dream of a completely controlled election rarely comes true. Into every campaign there are injected elements which threaten to upset the shrewd calculations of even the most perceptive leadership. A badly
maintained road may lead to a fatal automobile accident.
Teachers have been known to resign in disgust with the
state of the public schools. A group of citizens form an
indignant committee and take the campaign ball away
from the professionals. Any one of these things, and many
other incidents of the same kind, can force real policy or

program questions into the open. Then there is nothing much that the professionals can do except to improvise and make the best of things.

Experienced observers are inclined to believe, however, that there is a special clause in the law of averages which applies to political campaigns. In an amazing number of cases the injection of a factor injurious or helpful to one side is balanced by the appearance of another to offset the impact of the first, so that in the long run the politician who counts on the controlled vote comes out a lot better than one might expect. This is particularly true at the grass-roots level where issues are difficult to dramatize and personal contacts are at their most effective.

The Mass Media

When Franklin D. Roosevelt ran for President for the third and fourth times, 75 per cent or more of the newspapers in the United States opposed him. Yet he won handily on both occasions. This phenomenon led to a tendency on the part of the general public and politicians themselves to discount the impact of the mass media upon the political process. And largely on the basis of that experience there are still highly placed politicians who insist that television, radio, and the press do not significantly influence the results of an election.

The effective use of television by John F. Kennedy in 1960, the painful efforts of Hubert H. Humphrey to project an appealing personal image in 1968, and the touchiness of Vice-President Spiro Agnew about media coverage of the Nixon Administration suggest, however, that among men who know the situation at first hand the role of the several news distributing agencies is being taken with great seriousness. And when one studies the activities of the public relations firms which are increasingly managing political campaigns, he finds that their major emphasis is upon an effective use of television. Clearly at the level of national politics the mass media have come into their own as factors in shaping election victories. Since our primary concern here, however, is with grass-roots politics, we shall have to leave the analysis of national media to other commentators and concentrate on their role in local elections.

There is no question but that in this local area of political life the press is still the dominant factor in determining what happens at the polls. Not because of flaming editorials praising one party and condemning the other. (Such obvious polemics are very likely to backfire and produce results quite different from those sought.) But by the way in which the newspaper covers routine news about local events from day to day. It is generally recognized that reporters who get angry at the police department can create the impression of a crime wave by simply playing up every mugging and robbery that takes place in the metropolitan area. In the same way, newspapers which wish to promote a city administration or candidate can do so without ever mentioning the fact on their editorial pages. All they have to do is give dramatic coverage to the administration's achievements and play down its failures. And by featuring stories about selected individuals and their civic contributions they can make those persons politically important in the community within a short time.

Any observer of the political scene learns to detect this process in operation. A series of front-page stories about poor housing, discontent with schools, and probable increases in the local tax rate are obviously efforts to denigrate the party in power. Whereas, on the other hand, full coverage of a given candidate's criticisms and proposals makes it clear that the man in question has been tapped for political preferment.

The influence of the press is not always exercised in

such blatant fashion, however, nor is it necessarily manipulated in a politically self-conscious manner. The fact that certain kinds of local events always make the front page, that particular ethnic activities are relegated to the sports section, and that a certain discretion is used in reporting the escapades of young people with "proper" family backgrounds—all of these things make their long-run impact upon the attitudes of the community. And these, in turn, have a part in forming patterns of political response.

Something of this same role is played by radio and television. But since these media give very little space and time to local news events and tend to concentrate on the more dramatic national stories their influence upon grassroots politics is less direct than that of the press. They have their own impact. But it is more subtle and dispersed in its effect. It reflects itself in the transformation of the culture or in a filter-down influence flowing from their handling of national news.

Issue-Oriented Factors

In spite of the most vigorous efforts of traditional politicians to keep politics oriented around personalities and the various nonsubstantial factors that we have been discussing, issues of diverse kinds do keep intruding themselves into the political picture, even at the local level. This has always been true, but it is becoming more and more a common phenomenon every day. The development among Americans of a sense of national community has contributed greatly to this end. Two world wars, the advent of mass mobility, and the increasingly ubiquitous television set have made provincialism difficult to preserve. As our citizens begin to appreciate their common involvement in national and international problems that cannot be understood or solved by traditional personality politics, they inevitably become more aware of issues as such. This new consciousness serves as a source of political power in two ways:

1. On the one hand it constitutes a reservoir of support that can be tapped by any party or faction with enough imagination to see the opportunity. The most dramatic examples of this sort of thing in our recent history will be found, naturally, in national politics. In the thirties the Democratic Party very deftly used the tremendous economic changes through which the world was passing to consolidate itself as the majority party in the United States for many years. During the forties it was able to seize upon the international crisis to assert a kind of leadership that added to its lower-economic-bracket support the adherence of a great many middle- and upper-class groups that felt strongly about the Nazi threat to western civilization.

One of the interesting things to note at this point is that at the grass roots increased interest in issues still tends to express itself largely in terms of national questions. It is not rare to hear candidates for municipal posts deliver statements on Viet Nam or on the Federal debt. That the duties of their offices have little relationship to such thorny problems does not diminish their ardor. Thus, the voters of Sauk Prairie are allowed to choose between a candidate for sewer inspector who favors more ground troops in Indo-China and one who leans toward Vietnamization. We can only imagine the trepidation with which Hanoi awaits the outcome of such elections!

This sort of thing has small value in the democratic process except to reveal the politicians' awareness of the increasing issue orientation of the electorate. It would be a mistake to suppose that these Grange Hall orators really think that their opinions on foreign policy have direct importance. They are, for the most part, fully conscious that they are going through motions which have a purpose quite different from the apparent intent. That purpose is to satisfy an issue concern without discussing the questions that are immediately at stake in the forthcoming election. (There is a certain irony in the fact that many highly sophisticated Americans are encouraging this very kind of irrelevance by their single-minded concern for peace.)

The extent to which general appeals on abstract issues move any significant number of voters is difficult to measure. Some students of our politics are quite sure that issue discussion does little more than bring out people who might otherwise have stayed at home on Election Day, and that no significant number of voters choose their party or switch loyalties on this basis. Other commentators, with equal reason, argue that slogans and promises relating to dramatic issues can be used to produce critical changes in public sentiment at all political levels. There is no room here, nor for that matter enough wisdom, to settle this lively debate. Perhaps the best generalization with which to take our leave of it is this: Where national policy decisions are at stake people probably tend to be influenced significantly by discussion of issues. But in their behavior in local campaigns they are still primarily personality oriented. Thus, the utility of the open reservoir of issue concern is largely dependent on the specific situations in which it is to be employed.

2. There is, however, a source of power in particular issues that has not been covered above. This is the generation of pressure groups that work with varying degrees of effectiveness in support of those candidates and factions which seem most friendly to the groups' objectives. Here the power is derived not from direct and general appeal to voter concern but from the activities of the organizations brought into being by these concerns.

Pressure groups work in one or all of three ways:

1. They may operate in a fairly direct manner, holding national conferences, issuing policy statements, planting articles in newspapers and magazines, making pamphlet material available to clubs, schools, and business groups, and so on. These are the opinion-molding lobbies. Various foreign policy councils, economic-study organizations, and public-health foundations would come under this heading. Such groups rarely endorse parties or candidates, but by various means they are able to enhance the prestige of friendly individuals or factions. An invitation to appear on a Foreign Policy Association platform or an American Medical Association program can mean a great deal politically. Similar recognition by the local League of Women Voters or Civic Improvement Society can mean as much at the grass roots.

The difference between this kind of thing and the direct appeal of a politician to issue concern is that here the issue becomes merely the basis on which prestigious groups recognize the designated candidate. Thus, a happy compromise is achieved between straight personality politics and a substantive issue orientation. The lucky candidate is identified with the "experts" or "better elements" because his stand on a particular question has won their favor.

2. Pressure groups may operate in a somewhat more direct and obviously political manner. The great majority of them do so. These are the "lobbyists" in the strict sense of the term. They may engage in all the activities that characterize the first group. But they go beyond this and exert direct pressure on governmental bodies. Washington and the several state capitals swarm with such pressure groups. They make personal visits to legislators and administrators, appear before committees, organize "protest" letters from the folks back home, and in general keep their em-

ployers informed of what is taking place in areas of concern.

The approval of lobbies such as these can mean a great deal to any politician, and their opposition has often spelled serious trouble. The late Senator Richard Neuberger of Oregon reported the following experience at their hands:

While serving in his state legislature, Neuberger indicated support for a bill regulating the use of highway billboards. This, he felt, was long overdue, because public roads were literally hemmed in at many places by unsightly signs.

When word of Neuberger's stand got around, he was immediately set upon by lobbyists for the sign-board interests. Unions of sign painters denounced him as a foe of labor. Pathetic letters covered his desk pleading with him not to rob landowners of the small sums that they were able earn by renting space to advertising companies. He was even pilloried as an enemy of free speech.

This same story could be duplicated many times and even made to appear mild in comparison with others with the same theme. Government and the politicians who operate it are subject to inhuman pressures at the hands of a multitude of pressure groups. Candidates who play ball can be assured of reams of favorable publicity. Those who do not are given the ax in short order. Since these lobbies are remarkably nonpartisan, they constitute a ready supply of power for many varied political forces.

3. Finally, pressure groups can work in very direct ways through the most elemental political channels. Thus, the CIO has set up in many states a well-organized political action committee which functions on a county, town, and precinct level. It does most of the things that a political party does. It registers voters, canvasses neighborhoods, drives people to the polls, and endorses candidates for office. In return for this kind of support it expects, and often

receives, the right to influence party decisions on a wide range of issues.

Few pressure groups choose this direct method of operation. It requires a kind of dedication, manpower, and financing that they do not possess. But there are ethnic associations, patriotic societies, and professional organizations which do emulate this kind of grass-roots direct action in limited ways.

There can be no doubt that pressure groups play an important part in the structuring of political power in a democracy—particularly those which give direct and vigorous support to specific candidates. But obviously there has been in many circles a considerable exaggeration of their role, one which the pressure groups themselves are happy to encourage.

Americans, for reasons discussed earlier, are addicted to the conspiracy theory of politics. This makes us particularly susceptible to that bogeyman known as "the interests." We are inclined to believe that millions of innocent citizens cast their votes under the nefarious influence of the National Association of Manufacturers or that political parties have been bought up lock, stock, and barrel by the fabulous treasuries of the labor movement. More recently a composite villain known as the "military-industrial complex" has taken the center of the stage.

We have seen that there is a grain of truth to such theories. Businessmen and unionists, and undoubtedly military leaders as well, *are* engaged in efforts to influence the shape of national, state, and local policies. But the assumption that such cabals have overwhelming strength in politics is unrealistic. One of the constant complaints of men who run trade unions and business lobbies is that their members pay very little attention to them when it comes to making up their minds on political matters. Labor leaders in several states, for example, have seriously considered the complete abandonment of campaigning in local elections. They see some value in national electioneering because it serves as a platform for propaganda and education purposes. But they have begun to doubt that conspicuous labor participation in local elections has any real value.

In a sense the attribution of great power to "the interests" in politics represents an effort to deny the reality of class consciousness in the United States. Those who do not like to admit the existence of social classes with tangential, if not opposed, interests are somewhat embarrassed by the way in which election results tend to follow zoning lines in most communities. If workers and their employers have the same interests, if class is simply a Communist fiction, then how does one explain the divergence in affiliation of Republican "fat-cats" and Democratic "plebeians"?

The easiest answer has been shown to be "the interests." Labor unions mislead their people and drive them to the polls in dull-eyed masses to cast meaningless ballots. The Manufacturers' Association and the Chamber of Commerce fill their members' ears with hokum and get them to vote in response to the demands and advantage of a very specialized pressure group. There are no inherently opposed social classes and inevitable economic antagonisms in the United States, says our American mythology. It is all the work of nefarious schemers and power-hungry politicians.

The happy fact is that very few pressure groups can deliver their constituents' votes effectively, except on highly specialized issues. The obvious reason for this is that few people are members of only one power bloc. Most of us belong to a diversity of social, economic, and political groups. And the demands that they make upon us are always to some degree contradictory. As trade-union members we may favor legislation which will strengthen the bargaining power of unions. But as consumers we look with concern upon measures which will have an inflationary impact upon the economy. As taxpayers we applaud proposals for cutting government costs. But as parents we want good schools for our children. This list of internal personal conflicts is endless, and constitutes a kind of human balance of power which greatly complicates the efforts of interest groups to control our votes.

The sources of political power are too numerous and interrelated for any simple description and analysis. The involvement of one man in many social structures creates opposing pressures that complicate his own responses beyond hope of unraveling. The most experienced leader of the most sophisticated political machine is never really surprised when his calculations go wide of the mark. He understands that free men living in a complex social order cannot be finally allotted to or claimed by any allegiance. And, being a citizen as well as a politician, he frequently takes as much satisfaction as anyone else from this fact.

4

Joining a Party

Shall I join one of the major parties? Everyone who is active in politics asks himself this question from time to time. And the manner of its asking is strikingly similar to that of a small boy wondering whether he is ready to try the high diving board. Even in this day of violent confrontation and revolutionary rhetoric young people in the United States obviously find the prospect of party discipline terribly threatening.

This attitude is not too surprising when one stops to consider the atmosphere in which we are raised. Political parties and personalities tend to be regarded as creatures of the demimonde, along with sidewalk peddlers, race-track touts, and loose women. Joining a regular party organization seems at best an act of high courage and at worst a complete fall from grace. Parents have been known to threaten disinheritance or even suicide in the face of a son's or daughter's decision to go into politics. It is not uncommon to hear a clergyman express serious doubts about the possibility of remaining an ethical human being once this dangerous course has been embarked upon.

It should be obvious that this is a somewhat melodramatic approach to the problem. Political parties are equivocal organizations. They can become corrupt and in turn make corrupt demands upon their members. But mere party affiliation does not require the surrender of anyone's conscience. There are thoroughly honest men in the worst of the urban machines. They will probably never get very far into the upper ranks of leadership. But they are usually tolerated and given a chance to speak their piece along with everyone else.

As a matter of fact, some of the most experienced political observers testify that anyone who wants to protest against what he takes to be improprieties in organizational activity will get a better and more open-minded hearing in a political party than he is likely to receive in a large business enterprise. One who knows many politicians personally will not find this difficult to believe. It is a part of their professional equipment to be tolerant of differences and courteous to those with whom they disagree. (Today's enemy may be tomorrow's ally.) In addition, they know very well that the press is always eager to play up the complaints of an unhappy party member. For both personal and tactical reasons they are constrained to try to harmonize diversity in points of view, even that of a small minority.

Temptation is certainly in the way of those who try to be good party members. It is easy to rationalize unethical or even dishonest practices when the fate of an election hangs in the balance, and particularly when one is able to tell himself, quite truthfully, that the other party is doing exactly the same thing. In his eagerness to prove that he is neither naïve nor a prig, the political novice may be tempted to carry out orders that violate his sense of morality. Some of the most unethical and illegal undertakings in recent political history have been the work of enthusiastic zealots whose purity of intention was used to justify a multitude of sins. And there is something about the spirit of a political campaign, especially one that promises to be close, that can produce a kind of intoxication in even the most experienced veteran.

This is no reason for anyone's refusing to face the burdens of political responsibility. Temptation is an inherent part of life. Men were made to face it, not to hide from it. Those who shrink from association with their fellows in fear of temptation are rejecting one of the most precious attributes of their freedom as human beings.

The more significant facet of the question which opened this chapter is its tactical aspect. Can one *most fully* express his moral concern in politics by joining a party? Let us answer that question by first calling attention to some of the more obvious facts of political life.

When the average voter goes to the polls on Election Day he is given a choice between two men and two programs. If he has followed the pre-election campaigning, he probably has little use for either candidate and less understanding of either program. He has had no voice in the selection of the men and the formulation of the platforms. He holds his nose and votes for the lesser of two evils.

Q.: Who chose the candidates and wrote their campaign pledges?

A.: The men who run the two parties.

Q.: Who authorized them to do so?

A.: The rank and file members, either by explicit ratification or by failing to avail themselves of the appropriate means of dissent.

Here, then, is the answer to our question. The man who does not join a party has cut himself off from about 90 per cent of the decision-making that goes on in democratic politics. He has abdicated his power to set the level of personnel and the quality of platforms to those who *do* become active party members. And he has restricted his political influence to the barest minimum possible without actually ignoring the duties of citizenship entirely.

Which Party?

There are periods in history when no intelligent individual has any trouble making up his mind as to which of the two parties he ought to join. These are times when the philosophical cleavage between the parties is so great that a man is propelled into one or the other by the sheer force of his basic commitments. In the thirties, for example, it was as hard for a believer in strong central government to contemplate becoming a Republican as it was for a decentralist to join the Democrats. In 1964 the Goldwater take-over of the GOP re-created something of this same clear-cut division with the added fillip of the Senator's stand on Viet Nam to strengthen the antipathies generated by his nomination.

At other times, however, the two parties come so close to the center of the political spectrum that it is difficult to find passionate reasons for preferring one to the other. This was true during the two Eisenhower Administrations when a popular President with moderate views and a conciliatory temper managed to blur the harsh lines of old antagonisms and usher in an era of good feeling. During such periods the individual voter is not coerced by his political philosophy to choose or eschew either party and must cast about for some less emotional basis for his decision.

There are at least three primary factors to be considered under such circumstances:

1. There is the question of how the parties stand on important local issues. One may find that, despite their proximity on the national scene, they differ significantly over matters of great moment at the state and municipal

levels. Since we have entered a period of renewed emphasis upon local solutions to local problems this consideration must not be underestimated or overlooked in the process of choosing a party affiliation.

2. One needs to consider the possibilities of making himself effective in the party selected. Often one of the two organizations is far more open to new ideas and personnel than the other. This may be because it is the minority party or because its leaders are persuaded of the need for fresh blood in politics. Whatever the reason, the feeling that one will have a better chance of making his opinions count in one party than in the other is a perfectly valid ground for organizational affiliation. Of course, this decision can represent a kind of prima-donna psychology, and when it does it is a bad one. But the honest conviction that one can make a real contribution more effectively in this camp than in the other is a fair basis for selection.

3. It is always possible for one to feel an obligation to enter a party because it is weak and demoralized in his community. The two-party system cannot endure when one of the major organizations fails to play its part in maintaining a competitive situation. Repeated victory inevitably desensitizes the winning machine, making it less and less responsive to the wishes of the electorate. This also tends to set up a vicious circle in which ambitious young men drift into the winning party, thus reducing even further the effectiveness of the other party.

This course of action is not as quixotic as it may seem at first glance. While it is true that success normally breeds success, it is also true that in more subtle fashion too much success can set the stage for disaster. When one of the major parties grows fat and overconfident, a few determined people can often work wonders in reviving its prostrate opponent. A young lawyer in Michigan entered the Democratic Party some years ago in a community in which it appeared to have no future whatever. Today he is an important official in the Federal Government, following a series of dramatic political upsets in which he played a critical role.

Making a Political Debut

How does one break into politics? Perhaps the first thing to be said in answer to that question is that it is somewhat easier to do so today than at many times in the past. This is true for several reasons:

1. The mobility that has come increasingly to characterize our nation—the movement of people and industry, the decay of old communities and the rapid growth of new ones—has weakened many of the existing structures of political power. Party organizations that once held whole cities in their grip now find their position threatened by changing ethnic groups and shifting economic levels in the population. Cities and towns have been flooded with newcomers who have no deeply rooted party commitments and owe nothing to established leaders.

These social changes have opened up fissures in what had been the solid front of partisan organization and have created a need for leaders who are not now available among the faithful. In sheer self-defense political parties are being compelled to welcome or even recruit men and women for whom they once would have had very little use.

2. The rapidly growing complexity of society has confronted our party leaders with problems unlike any that they have had to face before. Crises in housing, schools, law enforcement, race relations, and so on, have made the job of governing unbelievably difficult. The men who once did an adequate day's work in City Hall now find themselves baffled, even frightened, by the demands made upon

them and are casting about for help from almost any source.

3. Finally, active involvement in politics is more easily undertaken today because of the dramatic new methods of campaigning that have been developed in recent years. The increased use of the mass media—radio, television, movie shorts, newspapers, etc.—has caused some deprecation of the traditional door-to-door campaigning technique. But this latter is still basic. It is just being used now in conjunction with more modern methods.

The end result has been to make party organizations eager for men and women who have some command of the new skills needed to run an effective campaign. Indeed, the political parvenu who happens to be telegenic may find himself climbing the ladder of political success with dizzying speed.

This, then, is at least as good a time as any for breaking into party politics successfully.

First Things First

It is difficult to make any generalization about the actual first steps in joining a political party that will apply to all organizations and localities. In some cases a new resident of the community hardly has time to unpack his clothes before a party worker is on his doorstep inviting him to the next meeting of the neighborhood club. In other communities the exact opposite is true. People have been known to make diligent inquiries about party membership, telephone offers of assistance to the organization, send in financial contributions at campaign time—and receive no response whatever.

In the months immediately preceding a recent Presidential campaign a colleague of mine moved into a new neighborhood. During the first week in his new home he received three telephone calls from different factions of the local Republican Party. Being a Democrat he thanked his callers for their interest, but preferred to wait for a chance to help his own party. When several weeks had gone by without any sound from Democratic headquarters, he telephoned and offered his services in the forthcoming campaign. His call was received with a kind of puzzled hostility, passed from one person to another, and finally dismissed with the assurance that someone would "get in touch with him later." That was the last word that he ever heard from the local Democrats.

The answer to these differences more often than not lies in the relative strength of the two parties. A party that is well entrenched in power and used to carrying the district is less likely to be interested in new members. It is doing all right. Why add more hands to share the credit and claim the favors? A party that is on the rise will have the opposite attitude for the opposite reason. Every newcomer means one more worker in a needy cause.

Let us suppose, however, that we are dealing with a community in which there is a fairly equal division of power. Sometimes one party wins; sometimes the other. In such circumstances both parties will be receptive to strangers, but not so eager for them that acceptance and advancement is inevitable. What is a reasonable course of action in such a situation?

The first step is to make an analysis of the political setup of the community. Occasionally this can be done through the publications of some civic group such as the League of Women Voters or the political action committee of a labor union. In some localities organizations of this sort have prepared very helpful pamphlets for the edification of new voters.

For the most part, however, information on the political facts of life must be gleaned from other sources. One of the best of these is likely to be the file of back copies of the local newspaper. The issues published in the weeks before an election are almost certain to give a fairly clear picture of the personalities and factional relationships in both parties. Wherever possible a personal conversation with an editor or political reporter should follow up the digging in the library. In almost all towns the gentlemen of the press know much more about the political process than they can publish, and they often give valuable information to one whose motives they trust.

Once the basic political alignments and power have begun to come clear, a little judicious talk with neighbors and local businessmen will begin to pay off. What one learns from such sources must be taken with some reservations. But without going overboard for any one interpretation or point of view, a reasonably intelligent person can deduce a good deal from a scattering of informal conversations. It is not *what* he is told that teaches him. It is the relationship between the *what* and the *by whom* that is revealing.

While engaged in the process of learning local politics, the novice should begin to make a name for himself in the community. This does *not* mean that he should express himself volubly on political matters. On the contrary, the less concern for such issues, the better, in this early period. First, because it is possible to make very serious errors in judgment on short acquaintance with any political situation. Second, because the American anti-political tradition tends to make people suspicious of anyone, particularly a newcomer, who seems to be taking issues too seriously.

The process of making a name for oneself is really remarkably simple in most communities. Parent-Teacher Association, Junior Chamber of Commerce, and diverse social and religious groups are excellent vehicles for getting to know and be known in the neighborhood. There is al-

ways a shortage of responsible and diligent leaders in these
organizations. The man or woman who has ideas and is
willing to work at them can become a figure of importance
in the average community in six months or less.

It is important to realize at this point, however, that
everything cannot be left to chance. One must often be
his own press agent and see that the most favorable light
is thrown on his contribution to whatever group he is serving. Here, again, the job is fairly easy. In all but the largest
cities newspapers are eager for information about local
events, especially when it is well written and easily trans-
posed into journalistic style. (It is appalling to discover
with experience how few organizations are able to submit
adequate press releases to the newspapers.) By sending
timely accounts of the activities in which one is engaged
to the appropriate reporter, a good deal of steady publicity
is possible on the basis of a reasonable amount of time
and work expended.

If anyone is offended by the suggestion that he publicize
himself in this calculated way, he had better give up the
notion of becoming effective in politics. Publicity is one of
the standards by which politicians judge the value of a
man to their organization. Most of what one reads about
local events in the press has found its way there by just
such personal initiative. It is the height of naïveté to suppose that the papers are filled with stories garnered by
disinterested reporters on the basis of their objective news
value. The truth is that most editors have far too few reporters available to do anything like a full coverage of
their area. They depend heavily upon receiving self-serving
items from a wide variety of sources. And they are seldom
disappointed.

The third step in this process of getting into politics involves making oneself a spokesman for some significant
part of the community on a matter of importance to it.

This is not a contradiction of what was said above about avoiding the discussion of issues. There is a great difference between generalizations about a variety of abstract or relatively remote policy concerns and a healthy interest in the condition of local streets, schools, or sewers. These to the average citizen are not "issues." They are problems. The man who can solve them is apt to stimulate a good deal of public confidence and enthusiasm.

A word of caution here, however. Frequently a person interested in attacking some local problem lets himself be drawn unnecessarily into assaults upon "the politicians" allegedly responsible for it. This simplifies the process of getting the press interested, and reporters have been known to encourage it. But it is very likely to create deep resentment in the very people with whom one hopes to work, both in solving the particular problem and in future political activity. It is far more effective, both in terms of the cause for which one is speaking and in terms of the ultimate goal of political participation, to act as an intermediary between discontented neighbors and the men at City Hall. Doing this need not involve any compromise with principle. It is a common and serious error to suppose that the only way to deal with a politician is to denounce him in public. My own experience has persuaded me that reasonableness and courtesy induce responsible reactions from most government officials.

It is time now to evidence an interest in party activity. This may be done directly by a visit to the local chairman. It may be done indirectly by letters to the press supporting the party in some controversial situation, or by a financial contribution at campaign time. The important thing is some visible gesture which aligns the individual with his party and indicates a willingness to serve.

Apprenticeship

In an earlier chapter we remarked on a political leader who still does much of his own clerical work in spite of the fact that he is one of the more influential men in his state. This is a clue to what the newcomer to organizational activity must expect when he signs up.

The foundation of political strength in America is in the neighborhood and in the contact between party personalities and the people up and down the street. This means that the most significant activity is that which builds up and maintains those personal associations and relationships. Far from regarding it as beneath his dignity to pass out handbills, collect absentee ballots, and drive people to the polls, the experienced ward worker realizes that these things will bear far better fruit on Election Day than the writing and delivering of learned discourses on the tariff. Such apparently minor functions win elections. And they build the personal influence of the man who carries them out.

This is one of the hardest things for the reform-minded intellectual to accept. He finds it almost impossible to see a relationship between his dreams of perfect democracy and the "Mickey Mouse" routines of which all democracy is composed. I have seen university students, for example, offer help in a political campaign, only to give reproachful glances and disappear forever when told what "help" meant! One of the reasons why seasoned politicians have so little fear of traditional reform movements is their long experience with the impatience of reformers when faced with the real job of politics.

The initial excitement of being involved in politics can give one a feeling of being part of a tightly knit organization whose members are all pulling toward the same end. Indeed, most of the public and semiprivate utterances of party leaders are intended to create just such an impression. It is easy for the newcomer to throw discretion to the winds at this point and take party unity at face value. This would be a serious mistake, however. Every political party is composed of various factions. These factions are usually engaged in a subtle tug-of-war for control of leadership positions. A great deal of time and energy goes into maneuvering for preferment and advantage. Often the rank and file of the party are unaware of the implications of these tensions. They are unwitting pawns to be moved to and fro by one leadership clique or another.

The sophisticated party member does not let himself be used against his will and better judgment. He may choose to align himself with one of the contending elements. Or he may try to remain above the conflict in order to serve larger organizational purposes. Whatever his course, it will be chosen with full understanding of what he is doing. He will not become the dupe of any faction. But it is not an easy thing for anyone to avoid becoming involved in the leadership and prestige squabbles that so often fragment political parties. The personality orientation of our politics gives such feuds a far greater importance than their substantial content would warrant. Many politicians find it hard to understand that there are people who care less about *who* runs the party than about *what* the party stands for. The man who tries to subordinate personality disputes to programmatic concerns will be looked upon as a queer bird indeed.

This is the very point, however, at which the responsible issue-oriented beginner may come into his own and make his first real impact upon party character. Although he will seem at first to be a strange or even suspicious phenomenon, he may very well elicit in the long run a kind of trust and respect that the chronic claquer never earns; for one of the perennial problems of politics is the eventual conciliation of the opposing sides in these internecine battles. Quarrels that rage violently between campaigns must either be settled before Election Day or take a heavy toll in lost votes. Frequently the resolution of the most destructive feuds is brought about by the leadership of those third-force personalities who stand for the centrality of program and concerted party effort on its behalf.

The Party Regular

Party work can be an absorbing and demanding activity. Indeed, it often tends to foreclose other interests and consume all the spare time of the one who takes it on. This should not be allowed to happen. Not merely for personal reasons, although they are always to be considered. But because complete absorption by routine party responsibilities can be self-defeating. As we have seen earlier, the value of an individual to his political organization is measured in large part by the kinds of contacts and following he has. These are not only necessary for original recognition. They also will determine the degree to which he is able to assert himself effectively on behalf of his convictions throughout his political career. The politician who loses touch with the groups from which he has in the past drawn his strength is likely to find himself in serious difficulty.

Maintaining Contacts

Many prominent national figures have learned the hard way how important it is to maintain contact with the grass roots. Recent political history is filled with stories of men who neglected to do so, to their lasting regret. A position in the Cabinet in Washington is an almost irresistible opportunity for ambitious politicians. It can also be a grave-

yard for them. The burdens of office and the limitations
which protocol puts upon their freedom of action in the
political rough and tumble often cost them their hard-won
roles in the party machine back home. It was the realization of this fact that made President Dwight D. Eisenhower wonder about the wisdom of Richard Nixon's remaining in the Vice-Presidential slot in the election of
1956. For the Vice-Presidency, like a Cabinet position,
can be a millstone around the incumbent's neck.

What is true of national politics is also true at the neighborhood level. The natural cynicism of Americans where
politicians are concerned makes them quick to detect or
imagine slights on the part of those to whom they have
given their support. When Mayor Richard C. Lee of New
Haven was involved up to his neck in the most complex
and time-consuming urban renewal problems, he was expected to keep up a continual round of visits to wakes,
lodge dinners, religious festivals, and a host of other social
events every week. No public official or party leader can
afford to neglect these basic contacts.

Party Discipline

One of the most popular of American myths is the assumption that the best candidate for office is the one who
can boast of his independence of all claims and ties. So
entrenched is this notion that a former member of Congress, who later became a state governor, once voted
against a particular bill just because he had been subjected
to a great deal of pressure to support it. He explained
quite candidly to a friend that he had no strong feeling
one way or the other about the legislation in question, but
felt that to oppose it in the face of powerful support from
clamorous groups back home would enhance his reputation as an unbossed, courageous, and independent person-

ality. He was quite right in his assessment of the situation, as subsequent events proved. This kind of thing makes it difficult for many people to understand the place and importance of party discipline in American politics. As a result politicians are subjected to a good deal of criticism when they subordinate their own opinion to the demands of party unity. Such compromises are often sneered at as cowardice or bowing to the yoke of the machine.

There are a great many times, however, when the individual who wishes to work responsibly within the framework of his party must go along with the organization even though he regards its decision as unwise. This is necessary because the only alternative is the fragmentation of political life and the elimination of all conscientious men from politics. Parties cannot formulate and administer policy unless they can be sure that their program will have the support of their members, especially those in legislative offices. If every politician always voted his personal opinion, democratic government would be even more chaotic than it is. In sheer self-defense we should be driven to the election of less righteous legislators!

It is easy to overdramatize the kind of concessions that must be made to party discipline. One tends to imagine them in terms of terrible sacrifices of principle. The truth is that they are rarely anything to get greatly exercised about. This is so for two reasons:

1. Most such compromises involve personnel rather than policy. One is asked to support for appointive or elective office some man who is less qualified than another. The personality and patronage orientation of our political life rarely lets party leaders get excited enough about issues to crack the whip on them. In six years as a municipal legislator I was never once *told* by my party leadership how to vote on any substantive matter. But I was expected to

support "the ticket" and the choices of the caucus for administrative positions.

2. The difference in qualifications between the official party designate and his opponent is rarely serious enough to warrant a rupture of the united front. The idea, fostered largely by fiction, that political leaders are constantly rejecting men of political genius in favor of corrupt barflies is wholly unrealistic. Very few of the former want to serve in underpaid government positions; and realistic politicians are shrewd enough to know that the latter are a poor investment in public relations. In academic terms it can be put this way: The party regular is sometimes asked to support a B-plus candidate over an A one or a C-minus over a C-plus. The choice is rarely between an A and a D. In fact, it is one of the characteristics of an able political leader that he does not expect his followers to make fools of themselves!

No man has a right to lead who has not learned to follow. This is as true in politics as anywhere else. The necessities of a complicated social and political mechanism call for an organized approach, not the sporadic assaults of a Lone Ranger. It is accurate to assert that the demands of party discipline rarely ask anything more in the way of sacrifice of integrity than do the requirements for success in any business or profession. An ethical man will be constantly troubled by the concessions that the presence and values of others force him to make. But he will understand that so long as he chooses to live responsibly in the midst of his fellows he must make such concessions, always conscious of their threat to his own integrity.

Favor Seekers

Years ago one of the nation's leading magazines carried a fascinating article by a young man who had become active in urban politics. The theme of his remarks was that he had found it almost impossible to avoid corruption at the hands of people who wanted favors done. The whole process, he pointed out, is very subtle. People will offer you bribes to do the things which they have every right to expect you to do. He was approached by individuals who were anxious to get licenses in order to put up overhanging signs, open taverns, operate veterinary hospitals, and so on. In almost every case the man asking for his intercession could have gone to City Hall, made formal application, and obtained a permit. When he suggested this simple alternative he was met with cynical glances, knowing winks, and sneers. His petitioners knew better! They were "wise to politics"! They understood that somebody had to be paid off for everything! For a time the writer of that article held out against this *quid pro quo* psychology. Eventually, however, he was persuaded by more cynical friends that his was an unrealistic position. He began to accept small favors in return for his services. And soon he was entangled in a network of ethically ambiguous relationships.

Every man who has had any experience in political life knows how subtle the temptation to misuse influence can be. It rarely comes in the form of classical villains in silk hats and cloaks demanding outrageous privileges and offering fabulous rewards. More often than not it is garbed in the dull aura of respectability, replete with church membership. What it asks in any specific situation is apt to be very simple, even reasonable. What it promises is seldom so enticing as to arouse suspicion. The worried father wants a word said to the prosecutor in charge of his hot-rodding son's case. He does not ask that the boy be exonerated, but that something be done to avoid "damaging publicity" and ease the fringe penalties of the law. A property owner finds that he is stuck with a piece of land that cannot be profitably developed under the town's zoning code. All that he asks is exemption from a few "highly technical" regulations. A local dairy owner would like the contract to supply milk to school lunchrooms. But he simply cannot meet the lowest competing bid. Surely a small enterprise, locally owned, deserves some concessions! And in return these men offer nothing, except contributions at campaign time and the fact that they are popular members of a large number of social and fraternal organizations.

The person who has grown up thinking of corruption in terms of large sums of cash passed under the table, obviously dangerous men, and clearly nefarious activities, can be taken off-guard by such simple requests. He will be tempted to use his influence in the party to help these decent people. Often this is just what he should do, through the proper legal channels. But it is important to remember that the essence of corruption is not the amount of money involved. It is the use of power to create inequities rather than remedy them. Every special consideration which gives one citizen a privilege not enjoyed under the law by all citizens is an abuse of public trust and can lead to more and more serious breaches of faith.

"A Man Who . . ."

One of the great sources of disappointment for politically enterprising young people is the discovery of just how few politicians ever become candidates for office themselves. In every community in the country there are able and ambitious men and women who have spent years working within a party without ever achieving nomination for office of any kind.

Available Candidates

This condition cannot be attributed simply to the low ratio of jobs to politicians; for many of those consistently passed over have qualifications more impressive than the men selected. The answer lies in the fact that a slate of candidates is expected to represent more than merely a collection of able men. Candidates for office must meet many tests that are only indirectly related to their potential effectiveness as public servants. They must represent the proper ethnic and religious backgrounds, claim membership in strategically balanced social groups, come from the correct geographic section of the community, and fulfill other criteria that are highly valued by the canons of American politics.

Thus, the opportunity of a given individual for nomination to office depends less on his talent and strength within the party than on his ability to show that he can supply something that the ticket will lack in voter appeal without him. This has tended to be the pattern in the past. But there is no reason to suppose that it will go on forever. The very fluidity of population that was discussed earlier is breaking down many of the group loyalties that were once so crucial. Some competent observers of the political scene fear that we may actually be developing a sort of homogenized American, one whose public image will be a kind of composite of all the qualities that we like to believe are characteristic of our populace at its best. There is even talk of the possibility of computers replacing conventions as techniques for selecting candidates!

Even if conditions never become so extreme, there is every reason to believe that with the passage of time political leaders will begin to realize that many of the traditional canons of selection must be radically revised or wholly discarded. Making this fact as obvious as possible may well be one of the major tasks of the present generation of newcomers to politics. Such a change in orientation would do more than merely widen the base of available candidates. It would also remove one of the major obstacles to public concern with substantive issues.

Shall I Run?

Those who are active in one of the major parties and possess the qualifications discussed above will eventually have to decide whether to accept nomination themselves. For some this will be an easy decision. The prospect will be so appealing or so appalling as to create no ambivalence. For others the answer will come only after a good deal of pondering.

Obviously there are no generalizations to be made here that can settle the matter one way or the other. A great many variables are involved that make such suggestions impossible. Personality factors, family status, financial capacity, the temperament of one's wife, the impact of the campaign on one's job—all these factors and many more must be taken into consideration. The decision is never easy. Men who are in every other respect excellent risks have been known to refuse because of the limitations of health. Others, as strong as workhorses, have had to refuse because they have found that their wives were not up to the demands made upon them by electioneering. The inevitable cost of the campaign sometimes casts the deciding vote. The fear of what may happen to his relations with customers or employer has made many a good man hesitate. All these are valid reasons for deciding one way or the other and need no further elaboration here.

There is, however, a further consideration that is too often overlooked in the excitement of being offered a place on the ticket or appointment to some administrative commission. Is this a job that will give one an opportunity to improve himself and continue to advance within the party and government?

It is not uncommon for parties to sacrifice a man in some position that is either unsuited to his talents or a complete dead end. This is sometimes done despite these consequences. Occasionally it is done *because* of them. Many a troublesome citizen has been taken off the backs of party leaders by relegation to a meaningless or unpopular post. One young man who was making a nuisance of himself on policy questions within his organization was elected to a place on the Public Safety Commission. Since this body is supposed to operate in nonpartisan fashion, he has been effectively removed from his previously critical role in party councils. Others have been similarly neutralized by being given seats on the board of education, civil service commission, or a technical planning committee whose work arouses little public interest.

Service in such positions must frequently be accepted, because there is a job to be done and the individual involved has the ability to do it well. There is no suggestion here that responsibility ought to be shrugged off under such circumstances simply out of concern for the political future. One will be well advised, however, to make sure that this is the case and not let himself be forced into a dead end for the sake of a balanced ticket or the removal of a thorn from the organization's flesh.

One final and important word on personal ambition in politics. At the grass-roots level the wise man never admits that he has no ambition for office or that he is content with the level of status which he has achieved. To do either of these things is to impair his influence within the party. In common with the rest of the human race politicians like to hitch their wagon to a star. They tend to rally around those figures who appear to be going places and align themselves with men who have a future. This is not difficult to understand, surely. The same practice is familiar in private business.

Once a man admits that he would not run for office if asked or makes it obvious that he has reached the peak of his ambitions, he becomes something like a lame-duck President. From that point on he begins to drift into the backwaters of the political stream, and his counsel, while it may be highly regarded for its wisdom, lacks the force of possible power. At the national level of our political life coyness and denials of interest in the White House have a traditional ritualistic value. It would be a serious mistake for anyone to try to enact that same ritual at the state and municipal stages of the game.

Crispin Crispian!

It was the first Tuesday in November. Election Day. *Five-thirty* in the morning. I drove through the streets of a still-sleeping town, across the tracks to the crowded tenements and flyblown storefronts of what we shall call the 50th Ward. A few people were hurrying along the sidewalks and others were stamping their cold feet as they waited on chilly corners for buses. This was the part of town where men started work at six and seven o'clock and might not take the trouble to vote unless carried to and from the polls.

When I parked in front of the Polish Eagles Club there was a dim light shining through the steamy windows and two cars standing at the curb, their idling motors sending out little puffs of vapor. There should have been many more. If the people of this area were to be voted in any number, we should need at least eight or ten—preferably a dozen—automobiles and drivers.

Inside the club, huddled near a woodburning stove, were

three people. The chairman of the 50th Ward, his brother-in-law, and a student named Bill Saunders. Bill had come to me two days before and said that he wanted to help out on Election Day. He figured that he could give about two hours. When would he be most needed? From six to eight in the morning, I had replied. And Bill was waiting when I arrived.

The chairman looked embarrassedly about our small group and muttered something about the people who would be along in a few minutes. We took our address cards and started out. For two frantic hours Bill, the chairman's brother-in-law, and I shuttled back and forth carting all sorts and conditions of men to the disgraceful old schoolhouse where the balloting was being done. Gradually we were joined by a few more party workers. They made cursory apologies for being late and spent much of their time setting up a percolator in the back room of the club. We could have used them on the streets, but that coffee did smell good when it finally started to bubble at eight-thirty.

I was surprised to see Saunders still there when I stopped by for some new cards and a doughnut at nine o'clock. He was to have quit at eight. But he backed up against the smoky stove and said that he planned to spend another hour and then leave. At eleven o'clock he was still driving. It was getting on toward the lunch-hour rush, he explained. He would help through noon and then take off. At three he was gently escorting a deaf and dumb couple into the polls, holding up two fingers to show them which lever to pull just as they went through the school basement door. It was barely seventy-five feet from the machines. Luckily no one in authority was looking at that moment!

I got caught in the four to six o'clock press and did not get back to the Polish Eagles Club until after the polls had closed. There was Bill Saunders sitting near the stove and drinking coffee out of a cracked beer mug. (The paper cups had given out about two o'clock.) He looked somewhat abashed to see me and explained elaborately that there would have been no point in going back to the library to study for two miserable hours at the end of the day.

When the votes were all counted our party had won in the state. It was an astounding reversal of every poll and prediction, and analysts tried to account for it in various ways. Some explained it in terms of economic factors. Others professed to find the answer in the personalities of leading candidates. A few spoke darkly of secret deals and stabs in the back. Probably all of those suggestions contained an element of truth.

There was another factor, however. One that is difficult to label. I find it simplest to think of it in terms of Bill Saunders, many miles from home in more ways than one, straddling a chair in the back room of the Polish Eagles Club, drinking coffee from a cracked beer mug and deciding to work "just one more hour." And I like to remember, too, the words of Shakespeare's King Henry V which seem so appropriate:

> And gentlemen in England now a-bed
> Shall think themselves accurs'd they were not here,
> And hold their manhoods cheap while any speaks
> That fought with us upon Saint Crispin's day.

Politics can be a wonderfully exciting business!

5

The Independent

It has often been noted that in the United States political independence is generally regarded as a primary characteristic of the virtuous man. Most Americans feel on the defensive about being affiliated with a major political party and hasten to assure one that they are really independent when it comes down to a particular election.

This antipathy toward party membership is a psychologically inevitable result of our reluctance to take politics seriously. The voluntarism which sees government as a necessary evil, something to be kept to a minimum and operated by people who have nothing better to do with their time, makes it equally difficult to see political parties as respectable parts of an important social process. They are, rather, suspected of being conspiratorial organizations largely concerned with getting jobs for their leaders and siphoning funds from the public treasury. Thus, to join a party is tantamount, in the minds of millions of Americans, to admitting that one has surrendered his heritage of individualism in return for some degrading advantage to position or purse.

The result of this attitude, as was pointed out in the preceding chapter, has been to keep the great mass of people from participating in the most significant part of the democratic process: the selection of candidates and the delineation of party positions on crucial public questions. This leaves the operation of most of the machinery of government to a small group of men and confronts the voters with severely limited options on Election Day. And this, in turn, sends the voters home smugly confident that they were wise not to have gotten more deeply involved in such a corrupt business in the first place!

The notion that one can express his ethical concerns only by abstention from, or protest against, traditional forms of political organization is one of the more unfortunate results of our denial of the reality of social structures. More often than not rejection of party affiliation is unworthy of the high motives to which it is dishonestly attributed.

As a tactic rather than as an absolute ethical principle, however, there is much to be said for political independence under some circumstances. When one refrains from identifying himself with a major party because he feels that it is possible to work more effectively for specific objectives in an independent position, his decision is not an effort to keep himself unsullied by the demands of party membership but a method of achieving ultimately more significant involvement in the political life of the community. This is a thoroughly defensible position and one that has been taken by many ethically concerned and realistic men and women.

Prerequisites to Independent Action

It is not an easy matter to outline the circumstances under which independence constitutes the most effective political strategy. The decision, in particular cases, must be made on the basis of local conditions, personality re-

sources, and the objectives that seem most important at
the time. There are some generalizations, however, that
may be helpful in reaching such a decision in specific situations:

1. Independent political action must eventually accomplish one of two things—either the conversion or coercion
of one of the regular parties or a portion of its members
or the establishment of a new political party. This is true
because ours is not a direct democracy. Decisions are not
made by counting noses or recording the volume of complaints on any one issue. Instead, decisions are made by
elected representatives who are put in office by a process
in which political parties play highly important roles. Unless the independent voter means to run a slate of his own,
he must manage to impose his program upon one of the
two principal political machines by which the functions of
government are borne.

Failure to understand this simple fact has led to the dis-
illusionment of many would-be political reformers. Over
and over again, a high-spirited political group sets out to
change conditions in the community and begins with loud
blasts against the existing political parties. It signs up indignant citizens, holds noisy protest rallies, solicits newspaper editorials praising its aims and deploring the evil
machinations of the bosses. For a while everything looks
hopeful. At last the parties are going to be put in their
places. Then, to the horror of honest citizens, one of two
things occurs. The independent group decides to run its
leaders for office or it "makes a deal" to support one of
the very parties it has been denouncing! In the first instance the chagrin of the died-in-the-wool independent
voter is great because he feels that his movement has been
turned into a vehicle for the personal advancement of a
few men. Somehow, our naïve citizen supposes, it should
have been possible to keep the reform movement com-

pletely out of politics. How such a totally nonpolitical group should have made its program effective is something that he does not feel capable of deciding.

Astute politicians are well aware of this dilemma of independent groups. They know that such organizations are going to have to come to terms with the political facts of life at some time or other. They are also familiar with the disgust that members of such a movement are apt to feel the moment their leaders stop making abstract generalizations about civic virtue and begin to implement a program of action. I have been told by cynical old "pols" that you can stop any reform group by slinging a little mud, accusing its organizers of personal ambition, and yelling "deal" when the time comes for it to support the opposing party or put up a specific slate of candidates. The "nice" high-minded, nonpolitical people who make up such movements just cannot stand having their sincerity questioned. They are strongly tempted to blame their leaders for having betrayed them and withdraw from further support of the organization.

2. Independent political action assumes the existence of a large group of interested but uncommitted citizens. Since it is necessary to influence the acts and aims of existing parties, there must be something to offer in return for the concessions that are being asked. Notice that there are two qualifying adjectives used in that first sentence, "interested but uncommitted."

3. It is almost impossible for independent action to succeed unless it has the support or recognition of the local newspaper. The reasons for saying this should be fairly obvious. Regular political parties, working on the principle of the controlled vote, do not always need publicity; indeed, they often thrive on the lack of it. Little publicity means a minimum of voter interest in political issues. And

this means a small, easily dominated voter turnout on Election Day.

An independent organization, however, depends for its success upon arousing the interest and indignation of the nonpolitical groups in the community. While this can be done by handbills and door-to-door visits, these devices are much more difficult to use effectively when the movement lacks the social infrastructure of the established parties. And there are a great many people who will have nothing to do with a "reform" organization that has not been baptized by liberal doses of printer's ink. The crusading editor is still one of the most popular symbols of truly independent political reform. An independent movement *can* succeed without him, but its task is immeasurably complicated.

4. One of the basic prerequisites to successful independent political action is the existence of issues which can be given a nonpartisan and nonideological orientation. School improvement, the elimination of administrative corruption, a better zoning code, and matters of this sort can often be effectively approached on such a basis. But questions of labor legislation, civil rights ordinances, welfare and relief programs, and things of that sort have tended to have become so identified with partisan positions and ideological patterns that it is very difficult to remove them from this context in most communities.

In the state of Rhode Island, for example, there flourished at one time an organization known as the Consumers' League. Under vigorous leadership this movement accomplished a great deal in the fields of labor legislation, pure food laws, and so forth. People of diverse political backgrounds took part in it. Republicans pressed along with Democrats for shorter hours for workers and cleaner conditions in dairies. Together they saw one campaign after another succeed beyond any reasonable hope. But in the

1930's the political climate of the nation, and with it Rhode Island, changed. Under the New Deal many of the issues on which the Consumers' League had worked effectively were made parts of a total social program that was defined in terms of party lines. Now Republican women who had supported the group when it fought for things such as child labor laws discovered that such things were "Democratic," "New Dealish," or even "Socialistic." Their enthusiasm waned. The result was a general deterioration of the organization and its eventual dissolution.

Independent political action assumes the existence of dramatic issues that have not been co-opted by either of the major political parties or by any clearly identifiable ideological faction in the community.

5. A strong independent movement demands an adequate supply of leaders with some experience in, and feeling for, the political process. The job of steering a middle course between the precincts of the regular political organizations is extremely difficult. This is particularly true in view of their eagerness to help the independent make a fool of himself. A few ill-considered press releases, blunders in approaching government officials, breaches of impartiality in dealing with the major parties, and a score of other traps await the inexperienced amateurs who set out to influence the politics of their town.

One such group destroyed itself in the first week of its existence by accepting the "kind offer" of the Republican Party to let it use a mimeograph machine . . . located in party headquarters! Another held its meetings in a labor union hall and lost half of its potential members that way. A third was ruined by the unwillingness of one of its committee chairmen to check the facts about the town charter before making charges and proposals.

The independent political organization will be the target of powerful attacks by all regular party organizations. It needs leadership of the most intelligent and sophisticated sort if it is to succeed.

6. Independent political action assumes the existence of real competition between the two major parties. Where there is a "double machine," *i.e.,* a permanent or passing agreement between the major parties on the limitation of issues, independent action is made extremely difficult. There are some communities in which the regular party organizations conspire to negate the impact of nonpartisan groups. They receive the delegations and suggestions of these movements courteously enough and then simply ignore all that is asked. Or they may refuse to have anything whatever to do with what one historic political boss called "them damned amateurs."

Our suggesting some of the basic conditions upon which independent political action depends is not meant to deny the possibility of success where all conditions are not present. Obviously, factors such as personality, public indignation, the health or senility of existing party organizations, regional traditions, and a host of others can create unique situations in which no general rule applies. While the aggressive independent need not be discouraged from launching his movement just because of the absence of some of the elements suggested, he ought to know why in his case the missing factor is expendable.

Principles of Organization

Let us turn now to a consideration of the principles governing the building of a successful independent political action project.

Paralleling Structures of Government

When thousands of American college students descended upon Washington, during May of 1970, to talk with members of Congress about the Cambodian incursion and related problems of foreign policy, they were almost invariably asked by those Senators and Representatives to whom they spoke what state and/or district they *voted* in. ("I know where you go to school, son. What I don't know is where you vote. I run for Congress, not class president.")

Some students were shocked and horrified to discover that many members of the two houses were not willing to talk to any but their own constituents and in a few cases refused to allow others even to enter their offices. The students felt that as citizens of the United States their views ought to interest all officials of government.

College students are not the only ones who fall victim to the assumption that politicians are moved by rational appeals or general threats emanating from people who have no claim upon them, except their common humanity. As often as not political reform groups make this same mistake. They are recruited from all those in the general vicinity who have an interest in the objectives sought, without regard to the lines of the election districts and party provinces involved.

One of the first principles of successful political action is recognition of the fact that politicians are more apt to be influenced by an angry housewife from their own bailiwick than by a host of angels from the next town. Thus, the effective organizing of an independent group depends upon building along lines closely parallel to those which political parties recognize and by which they themselves are governed. No matter how tempting it may be to accumulate members without regard to the apparently arbitrary divisions of precinct, ward, county, etc., the wise organizer will insist upon voting areas as the basis for the movement's structure. Anything else is little more than a propaganda or educational association.

Representative Base of Membership

It is said that when two laborers were elected to the vestry of a large Episcopal church in New York, a distinguished financier who was also a vestryman expressed personal dissatisfaction with their selection. He had hoped, he said, that the vestry would always consist of the kind of gentlemen that he could invite to meet in his library! Such an attitude shocks us when applied directly to the affairs of the church. But it is not at all uncommon in political action groups. The words "the sort of people who could meet in my living room" have been used more than once in discussing the make-up of a potential community organization.

The temptation here is not difficult to understand. Most of us see the community through the eyes of our activities and friendships. We easily come to think of certain types of individuals and particular people as representative of the best and most responsible thought. Thus when the time comes to organize anything from a bridge game to a reform drive, we are likely to think first, and often last, of the old familiar faces.

It is not an easy thing to approach persons or groups with whom one has had little or no contact, particularly with a proposition that requires a good deal of trust in the one making it. Nevertheless, it is a necessity in political action. Geographic spread, social group representation, religious variety, and political sympathy are all considerations that should guide the invitation to participate. Only by acquiring a representative base can any group truly claim to be a spokesman for the whole community.

Sound Publicity and Public Relations

It has been suggested earlier that one of the most effective devices by which political parties combat independent action in their communities is by misrepresentation of the motives and activities of the new group and its leadership. One who has had no political experience will find it hard to appreciate how true this is. The public is particularly susceptible to all such calumny, partly because of its cynical suspicion of all political activity and partly in resentment against what seems to be in many cases a self-appointed custodian of public morals. Thus, well-planned press and public relations are of the utmost importance. The community at large must be apprised of the nature and purposes of the new organization in such a way as to minimize opportunity for misunderstanding. This does not take a staff of experts. It does take a sense of the public mood and some imagination.

Often this aspect of the whole business can be handled in close conjunction with the editors or reporters of the local press. In many towns newspaper publishers have served as enthusiastic consultants to civic reform groups, assisting them in every way to make the best case for themselves in the eyes of the public. But this responsibility, whether handled by an experienced professional or turned over to an amateur enthusiast must never be carelessly borne. It can make or break the group.

Careful Timing

The fatal weakness of many efforts at independent political action is a hasty birth precipitated by some crisis or scandal in the community. While many organizations that have been generated spontaneously by public indignation or fear turn in an excellent job on a single issue or election, a far larger number of those that are badly timed fail completely.

There are two kinds of mistakes in timing that can

seriously injure the chances of any political action program:

1. Mistakes vis-à-vis recruiting possibilities. Efforts to
organize independent political action in the week following the United Fund drive when every civic leader is exhausted from doorbell ringing, or in the middle of June
when everything is slowing down for the summer, or two
weeks after a disastrous election when no effective action
is possible for at least a year or possibly two. The list of
timing mistakes of this sort is almost endless. People must
be caught at a moment when their energy and enthusiasm
coincide with the opportunity to act promptly in some sat-
isfying way.

2. Many errors are made relative to issues. In a small
New England town, for example, a group of citizens had
become disgusted with the way in which the schools were
being treated. Budgets had been cut, teachers overloaded
with work, and buildings allowed to deteriorate. Nothing
in the way of organized action had been undertaken, however, until the word went out that the Board of Education
was going to require a loyalty oath from all school personnel. Outraged, the people who had been only muttering
up to that time went into action. They formed a committee
intended to stir up interest in the whole education problem
in their town. The result? They were denounced loudly as
"Red lovers," lost all chance to do anything constructive,
and soon thereafter broke up.

This was terrible timing. We may admire the spunk of
such people but cannot approve their judgment. If they
had been concerned chiefly with the loyalty oath, they had
every right to organize when they did. But to let themselves
get out on that frail limb in their first public appearance,
when their real concern was much more broadly based,
was a bad mistake in timing.

A group that wants to make its voice heard and listened

to with respect must introduce itself to the community at the most propitious time possible. This may be in the days leading up to an election when it can pose pertinent questions to the candidates of both parties. It may be when some popular clamor needs an articulate spokesman. Or it may come at a time of apparent political calm when the new group can introduce itself by interesting but noninflammatory inquiries into the operation of local government units. The important thing is to select a moment when the possibility of being accused of special pleading or ulterior motives is at a minimum.

Strong Planning Core

It is almost inevitable with independent political groups that their leaders be disciples of the democratic method carried to fearful extremes. A desire to avoid the very sort of "boss rule" that they are trying to fight in the major parties often misleads reform movements into an effort to operate in completely undisciplined fashion. Meetings are disorganized and much too long. Members get a feeling of aimlessness. Conflicting and overlapping assignments sap the time and energy of all concerned. This is no place for a discussion of how to conduct a good meeting. But it can be said that anarchy is not the answer. No matter how sophisticated its membership, a group operates with greater over-all effectiveness, creativity and ultimate democracy when its work is laid out by careful advance planning. This need not foreclose vigorous debate of policy decisions. It can actually make such debate more fruitful. And far from seeming to discourage democratic participation, it can guarantee a maximum amount of it by assuring members of the most reasonable use of their time.

Democracy does not work by insisting that disorganized masses generate detailed programs. It operates, rather, by putting responsibility in the hands of able leaders and giving the whole group the right to accept, amend, or reject their proposals.

Caveat Elector

There are a great many more things that could be said about the problems and techniques of independent political organization, but there is no room to go into them all. Let us close this section, therefore, with a few caveats:

1. Prominent names are necessary for window dressing. It is unwise, however, to expect much routine work from people who have their fingers in a dozen different pies. The men and women that you are told you "must get" are probably the ones on whom you will be able to count the least. Although they may have been dependable workhorses at one time, many of them will feel that they have served their apprenticeship and are ready for advancement to the letterhead of some dignified organization. Look for the young men and women with more zeal and time than fame.

2. Political parties will not hesitate to use independent groups as the means by which to attack their opposition. Frequently "public spirited" members of one of the major organizations will offer "the real low-down" on the other party. Listen to such information, but be very careful about believing or acting upon it.

3. There is always a tendency on the part of independents to denounce politicians. Sometimes this is justified and necessary. Often it represents nothing more than a feeling that reformers are supposed to act that way—at least they do in the movies! Frequently the politicians that we condemn out of hand are giving us better government than we deserve. A little reasonableness in speaking to and

about the leaders of the major parties may pay off in many surprisingly helpful ways.

4. Real grass-roots political action does not have to cost a lot of money. Any proposal that necessitates a large expenditure should be examined with great care and some suspicion. Far too often spending money is an easy substitute for the real business of building an organization from the ground up. Those who have had experience in successful political reform movements have frequently noted, with some surprise, that their principal expenses were for postage stamps, telephone calls, and mimeographing. Beware the glossy pamphlet, mass meeting, and big-name banquet. These are devices of limited usefulness. It is a serious mistake to devote time and effort to raising money for such projects that could more profitably go into neighborhood organization. You are after votes, not prestige.

5. Two last words. First, independents are often dismayed by the tendency of their associates to use the publicity that they get through nonpartisan political action as a springboard into party politics. If there is reason to suppose that an individual has joined the group simply for that end or that he is misusing his relationship to the group's detriment, this is reprehensible. A sharp eye should be kept out for such opportunists.

Frequently, however, sincere men and women become involved in independent activity because they have been unable to find an effective means of breaking into party organizations or have been unwilling to align themselves with existing party leadership. If a change of circumstance makes joining a party appear more feasible or desirable, this should not be held against the individual involved. Indeed, sometimes the one benefit to the community of a reform movement is its tendency to encourage a kind of political awareness which ends in the acceptance of party responsibility by more people.

Second, with the passage of time an independent group will often find itself more and more frequently aligned with one or the other of the two major parties. Theoretically this should not be true. The independent organization is supposed to pick and choose candidates for its support on the basis of their fitness and without regard for party label. But one learns quickly in politics the importance of integrated programs and interpersonal teamwork. If one of the parties makes a real effort to attract the independent vote by nominating basically competent candidates and offering platforms which are fundamentally acceptable to reform-minded people, the temptation to support that party down the line is very great. It begins to seem moralistic in the worst sense to split up a municipal administration, for example, merely because of relatively minor differences in individual candidates' qualifications.

The same thing is likely to occur with respect to issues. Either the Republicans or the Democrats may assert such vigorous leadership in meeting major problems that the independent movement becomes first psychologically and then organizationally committed to one or the other. When this occurs, the best policy is often to acknowledge that the need for that particular reform drive has passed, that its basic objectives have been fulfilled, and that it might as well close up shop and advise its members to take their places in the ranks of party workers.

In short, it is as important to know when to end such a venture as it is to know when to begin it. An organization that winds up its activities when its work has been completed enhances the reputation of its leaders and leaves them in a strong position to rally the troops again should the need arise.

6

Hitting the Campaign Trail

Political campaigns at the state and national level reflect increasingly the mechanized specialization of our age. Several prosperous public relations firms throughout the country devote full time to the planning and conduct of political campaigns. They begin with an analysis of the candidate's personal image, refashioning what nature did imperfectly, and plot the whole course of his campaign, including his stand on the most crucial issues. Those who run such enterprises tend to take a highly professional view of politics. They hire themselves out to any person or party that can meet their fees. And their recommendations on issues have little to do with the private views of their operators.

The prevalence of such "packaged" campaigns has stirred up a great deal of indignation at all points on the political spectrum from right to left. And there are real questions as to what this trend implies about the health of the democratic process. Whatever may have been wrong with the torchlight parades of the past, they at least had the virtue of being clumsy enough to falter at critical points and allow the voters to catch a glimpse of what lay behind the façade. Modern computerized techniques have eliminated many of the traditional gaucheries. And the slick product of a Madison Avenue team often seems able to walk through an entire campaign without ever becoming fully visible, either as a person or as the spokesman for a substantive position on public questions.

Despite the moral outcries of their opponents, however, professionally managed candidacies are bound to become more rather than less common. And where once they were largely limited to the highest offices in the land, they are beginning to appear in even relatively insignificant electoral contests.

There is little point, therefore, in taking space in a book of this kind to discuss large-scale campaigns for major political office. Even where no highly specialized public relations firm is employed, the techniques which they have developed are being adopted and used by candidates who have the incentive and backing to spend large sums of money on their campaigns. The man who wishes to run for Congress or the statehouse will inevitably need and get far more detailed and sophisticated counsels than can be offered here.

At the local level, however, which is where most politicians get their start and where, as indicated earlier, significant power bases are established, campaign procedures are still relatively "amateur" in character—that is, they are run by the candidates themselves with the assistance of a few personal friends and party workers and are a composite of traditional methods. It is this local level campaigning, then, about which we may helpfully speak to those who are newly come to the great American game of politics.

Getting Ready to Campaign

Let us suppose that you have been nominated for some local office by the regular organization of your party or have won endorsement by victory in a primary election. In either case your first move should be to attempt a rapprochement with those who opposed your selection. Obviously this will be more easily undertaken where there was no primary and the differences of opinion within the party were worked out through "normal" channels. Even in such cases, however, it would be a mistake to suppose that the job of reconciliation is unnecessary. The American tradition of reticence about pushing too hard for public office is so strong that even in local politics men and women who have served the party well often expect that they will be offered an opportunity to run for office without having to press their claim vigorously.

It is not at all uncommon to find very deep bitterness behind an apparently unanimous party decision. And the animosity of a man who has been snubbed can be as deep where he made no gesture of interest in the nomination as where he ran a strong and open race to get it. One party chairman, after presiding over a nominating meeting at which only one name was even offered, got word that one of those present at that session had left vowing vengence for what he considered an unforgivable slight, *i.e.,* his name had not been put before the group.

"What the hell did the so-and-so want us to do," the chairman raged, "beg him to allow us the privilege of nominating him?"

Apparently so. And the wise candidate makes it a point to visit anyone whose nose may be out of joint as a result of his victory. Such calls are valuable from several points of view. They patch up quarrels, build useful alliances, provide the candidate with many excellent tips about the nature of both his own party and the constituency in which he is to run, and, not least, indicate to party leaders that he has foremost in his mind the unity of the whole organization.

My own first nomination to the Board of Aldermen of the City of New Haven won the tentative approval of my ward leaders. That tentative approval turned to enthusiastic support when my predecessor in the job was generous enough to give me *his* friendship. He gave me more than mere friendship, however. He prepared a map of the ward marked with helpful indications of ethnic and economic status, took me personally to visit his friends, and arranged several meetings for me with influential groups in the neighborhood. And all of this because I called upon him after my nomination and courteously asked his assistance. Late in the game, when we had become good friends, he admitted that if I had "come on like some tough politician trying to browbeat" him into supporting me, he would not have given me "the time of day."

Another way of saying this is that a new face in a position of influence in the party tends to threaten many people. They fear the loss of their own status and prestige. An honest effort to assure them that he is not out to tear apart the old structures and relationships will be well worth the time of any new candidate.

When nomination has been wrested from an opponent in a primary election the task of re-establishing the lines of communication is in some respects harder and in other respects easier. The greater difficulties are obvious. Your antagonist and his supporters have worked hard and spent money to win the primary and have lost. Unless they are superhuman vessels of forbearance they will be bitter about their defeat and angry at you, no matter how properly you may have conducted yourself in the campaign. They will be tempted to "sit on their hands," as the press loves to describe this tactic, and allow your opponent in the inter-party election to give you a well-deserved beating.

On the other hand, the very fact that the matter was thrashed out in an open contest and settled by a majority of the members of the party makes it a bit harder for your late opponent to rationalize his resentment in terms of secret deal, stab in the back, and unholy alliance. Those to whom he goes with such tales are far less likely to believe him than if you had been selected in a closed caucus of party leaders. In addition the prominence of the primary will have focused the spotlight of public attention on his behavior. If your defeated foe hangs back in the subsequent campaign and fails to carry his share of the burden as a loyal party member, he inevitably puts himself and his friends in a bad light and weakens their position in the future. Party leaders can forgive a man who simply lacks enthusiasm for *their* choice. But they tend to be hard on the one who exposes the party to the turmoil of a primary and *then* is not big enough to accept its outcome.

Give your late opponent every face-saving opportunity! Turn the other cheek. Walk the second mile. Forgive at least seven times. Let him work out his bitterness. Then reach out for his hand. And with amazing frequency you will have won a friend.

The second step in getting ready to campaign is to do some intensive homework on the history of past elections in your ward, precinct or town. How has the vote fallen in previous contests? Where is your party's strength? Its weakness? What kinds of men have won? What sort of campaign have they waged? Which issues seem of most interest to those for whose votes you are going to bid? Does a large vote favor your party or the opposition?

If you are fortunate enough to have an efficient party organization, this kind of information and a great deal more will be available to you in its archives. A good ward chairman, for example, will have records which tell him who voted in recent elections, at what hour of the day each voter can be expected to appear at the polls, and which enable him to know early in the day whether the total turnout is going to be large or small. In addition he will have lists of invalids, chronic travelers, men and women in service outside the state, and others who will need absentee ballots. A *really* first-rate organization can also predict the way in which each voter is likely to throw his support in a given election. Not because it engages in any illegal snooping or coercion, but because its block leaders have done their work well and are sufficiently acquainted with their neighbors to make a reasonably accurate forecast.

Where the party is not able to provide this kind of data you will have to dig it out from the files of local newspapers, which are available at the public library and in the offices of the journals themselves. Anyone with a sufficiently developed political instinct to be nominated will have little difficulty doing a quick brush-up on his constituency by studying the statistics published the day after each previous election. And if the office sought is a major one (*i.e.,* one that involves city- or county-wide issues), some reading of pre-election newspapers will give useful insights into the factors which led to the results tabulated.

Detailed information about a smaller electoral district such as a ward or precinct is rarely given in the press. Only where such a political subdivision is expected to be a "swing" factor in a close vote or where it is the locus of some especially crucial contest, as that between two obvious "comers" on the political scene or the emergence of a new ethnic power, will you learn much about your area from the daily newspapers. (It is one of the early disappointments in a budding political career to discover how little attention is paid to those candidates who are not at the head of the ticket!)

In the absence of help from party files or newspapers you will be forced to rely on the oral tradition—that is,

on the observations of those men and women who pride
themselves upon knowing the community in which they
live. Fortunately those who collect such information tend
to delight in sharing it. They rarely hide their knowledge
under a bushel. Once you have located the neighborhood
patriarch or matriarch and got him or her talking your
biggest job will be to get away without giving offense and
evaluate what you have been told.

Such an evaluation is not too difficult. Obviously what a
man tells you about his own ethnic, religious and racial
community will be far more dependable than what he has
to say about strangers. (And it is important to remember
that in addition to being loquacious neighborhood scribes
are often so intensely loyal to their own kind that they cannot be trusted too far in their comments about "out-
siders.") But beyond the obvious limits of group membership there are other criteria for judging the worth of what
one is told. Gossip has a way of betraying itself, prejudice
uses a vocabulary of its own, which one quickly learns to
recognize, and cross-checking the counsels of different
people becomes almost second nature to the maturing politician.

Listen to everyone who will talk to you about your constituency. But reserve judgment about the worth of what
is said until you have what statisticians call "an adequate
sample."

A word of special warning at this point. You will be
well-advised to avoid letting these exploratory conversations become sessions in which you commit yourself to
positions on particular issues. Some of those to whom you
talk will try to draw you out about problems which interest
their friends and themselves. You cannot, and should not,
avoid discussions of such matters. But remember, you are
there to solicit information and advice. You have every
right to refuse, albeit gently, to respond to questions with

firm commitments. People more often than not respect a politician who insists upon getting all sides of an issue before taking a stand on it.

The third step in your pre-campaign preparation should be the compilation of a list of those friends, party workers, and sympathizers upon whom you can count for assistance of a practical kind. Do not assume that nominal party members, even officials, will automatically be enthusiastic laborers in your vineyard. What was said earlier about the nature of political parties should prepare you for the discovery that for many people being active in a party means everything but working in an election! For good and bad reasons only a few of those who technically make up the "organization" and govern its councils between campaigns will really pitch in and do the grubby work of getting out the vote. The rest will talk a good game and can easily mislead you into imagining that they are doing what they promise. Many a beginner has discovered on Election Day that much of what he assumed had been well taken care of had not even been touched. So you will have to build your own working staff. And you will have to do this without offending the sensitivities of those who are theoretically the foot soldiers of the oragnization. This can be a very touchy business. Everyone knows that many party stalwarts talk more than they work. But this fact is not discussed openly in polite political company. And any effort to insinuate a cadre of "newcomers" into the ranks of the organization will be deeply resented.

The standard procedure for solving this problem is to have some personal supporter who is not an active party leader form a "Volunteers for ———" In it you can enlist all those whose primary concern is your election rather than the preservation of their personal fiefdom within the organization. These are the people who will do most of the legwork of the campaign. And many of the party regulars will co-operate happily with them. Such volunteers are, according to the protocol of politics, a nice group of bumbling amateurs whose energies will be useful in a limited way, provided they do not get underfoot! It is often galling to have to maintain this fiction, to have the real workers condescended to as dilettantes by those who do less than they do. But in fairness it must be said that there is here a reasonable division of labor. Many of the volunteers who carry the burden of the campaign battle want nothing to do with the routine housekeeping chores of the party between elections. Once you have won or lost they return to their personal interests and leave the important inter-election work to be done by the professionals.

So enlist your friends and personal supporters from inside and outside the ranks of the organization. You will need both and had better be prepared to spend time maintaining harmony between them.

Fourth, check into the election laws covering your city and state. This may be done quite simply. Your party chairman should know them and be able to brief you on your obligations. If he is uninformed (and he may be), a visit to the office of the appropriate election official will in all probability give you the necessary information. Where you are involved in a particularly bitter campaign it is sometimes wise to have a friendly lawyer review the advice that you receive. Even responsible holders of public office have been known to omit "accidentally" details of legal procedures about which they have been asked by members of the opposition party or faction.

The kind of thing on which you will need to be advised is the legal requirement concerning your campaign agent or treasurer, the provisions in the statutes regarding the solicitation, disbursement and recording of contributions, the amount of money which may be spent on your campaign, and the dates on, or by which, such data have to be filed. Most communities have regulations governing these matters, and you will need to be acquainted with them.

Fifth, in the pre-campaign period you will want to get copies of the voter list for your district. In most areas this will consist of three different sheets: the entire roster of those registered, the list of those registered as members of your party, and the one for the opposition party. This last is not always easily come by. But a bit of persistence will usually produce results.

Once you have the three lists in hand note on the master sheet the party affiliation of all those who are shown on the two party primary rolls. (As a practical matter you will probably have been given several copies of each of these lists and will have a variety of uses for them.) This will show you something about the make-up of your constituency and the kind of campaign that you will have to wage. In the average American community the great majority of those registered as voters will not be party members. They will be independents, which simply means in many cases that they do not want their party affiliation made public and are willing to forego participation in primaries and other party activities in order to preserve privacy.

If the two major parties stand at anything approaching equal strength, you may discover that one of them has enrolled a far greater number than the other on its primary list. You should not be unduly encouraged *or* discouraged by this fact. It often means nothing more than that one of the two organizations has been more zealous in its solicitation of voter enrollment, usually as a result of some recent intraparty dispute. There are cities in which the registered Republican vote, for example, is only a fraction of the Democratic list, but in which the Republicans regularly win elections. And there are suburban communities in which the opposite is true.

As your campaign begins to roll, you will find these lists invaluable and will want to annotate them with various kinds of data. They will be the real key to the effectiveness of your campaign. If the voter registration laws of your community allow late periods of enrollment, it will be necessary to secure supplemental or revised lists as they become available. Do not neglect this task. Those who register late are likely to be newcomers to the community or young people who have just reached their majority. Such voters tend to be more open to persuasion than the old-timers. And they are likely to respond to issue-oriented appeals. So keep track of them and approach their door with this fact in mind.

One of life's most rewarding sights is a voter list filled in with the various symbols which indicate a careful analysis of the constituency. Happy is the candidate who can stand before his work table on election eve and gaze down at a sheet fully covered with multicolored checks!

Finally, draft a campaign leaflet calculated to appeal to what your analysis shows is the nature of your potential support. As you begin this process remember your own habits in reading such material. What do you do with junk mail? Probably toss it into the wastebasket with no more than a glance. How about the soap premium offer that is slipped under your door? Unless you have a thing about soap, it probably goes into the circular file also. Your neighbors are like you in this respect. They are so deluged with slick commercial appeals that they have learned to discard them with minimum attention. So make your campaign leaflet different enough to be noticed. This is not so difficult as it seems. Here are some hints on how it can be done:

1. Choose a paper with the color and texture that announce it is not ordinary advertising. Obviously I am not suggesting "shocking pink." There are off-whites, light tans, and other tints which tend to stand out from the day's second-class mail. Pick one of these tints and try to get a somewhat textured paper, something that has more the quality of an invitation than an announcement. It is surprising to discover the degree to which the "feel" of a brochure can call attention to it.

2. Make use of a somewhat different shape. Commercial mailings are generally cut to fit easily into standard envelope sizes. A square or almost square leaflet will be a bit more inconvenient to "stuff" when the time comes for mailing. But that very fact will give it an edge in the fight for attention.

3. Keep the printed material brief and have it set in fairly large type. A good picture of yourself goes on the front with a list of your primary biographical material and qualifications for office below it. For the reverse side you can make your pitch on one or two of the critical problems of interest to the voters. Here you will need to use smaller type and narrower margins. But only those who are sufficiently motivated by the face of the paper will bother to look at the more detailed paragraphs on the back of it. You can afford to make them work a bit harder to get what is there.

4. Have your printing done at a union shop and be sure that the so-called "union bug" is shown on it. Anti-union voters will pay no attention to its presence. But its absence can be a real embarrassment among union members.

You may as well be realistic about the function of this leaflet. It is not going to educate the voting public, nor is it going to persuade them by its logic to support you. Its primary task is that of an introduction, to be for the local candidate for minor office what the press conference replete with buffet luncheon is for the head of the ticket. The data contained on its face should be aimed at making the voter aware that a man named So-and-So is running for a specific office, so that if and when he sees your press releases or other mailings later in the campaign he will be more likely to pay attention to them.

A little sophistication in designing your brochure will not be amiss. People are getting a bit tired of the use of nicknames, simplistic slogans, and photographs of the candidate's family, including pets. Do not automatically use such devices just because old campaigners advise it. Know yourself, your personal appeal, and the make-up of the community well enough to judge these techniques by their value to your campaign.

The Campaign

It is important to remember throughout your campaign that some of what you must do is intended less to sell you to the voters than to keep up the morale of your own troops. Several of the time-honored electioneering devices still in use do not add one vote to the candidate's electoral stature. But they do entertain and inspire the people who *can* by their efforts bring in a great many votes.

Under this heading I would put the neighborhood coffee hour or tea, the "Monster Rally" at which beer is served and door prizes handed out, and the leg-weary hours which many candidates spend pacing up and down outside the polling place on Election Day trying to win last-minute conversions by quick handshakes, just beyond the off-limit area. Such activities as these are almost always cases of preaching to the converted. Those who attend political rallies are invariably the party faithful. The courteous men and women who sip coffee while the candidate discusses the school budget would not have come had they not already decided to support the speaker. And anyone who lets himself be won as he walks through the door into the polling place should be disenfranchised!

The real function of these activities is organizational. The coffee hour may be used to recruit active volunteers from among passive supporters and encourage others to make financial contributions to the campaign. The party rally stirs the spirits and injects something like the scent of victory into the autumn air, thus encouraging the troops to give a little added effort. And no candidate who has ever walked his beat outside the polls will deny the value of this ritual once he has seen the pleased smiles on the faces of those who are bringing voters to cast their ballots. The sight of "our man" fighting right down to the line for every last vote is obviously important to all party workers on the day of battle. It would be a mistake, however, to overestimate the vote-getting power of such traditions in themselves.

Campaign Headquarters

What you should plan on in the way of a campaign headquarters will vary with the character of the office sought and the size of the area to be covered by the campaign. If you are running for the City Council from one small ward among many, it is pointless to rent commercial space for the length of the campaign. You may wish to do so for the week immediately preceding Election Day. But you can save money and lose nothing if for the bulk of the time you work out of a room in your own home. There is, in fact, a convenience to having your headquarters always at hand, and unless your home is calculated to stir awe and envy in your supporters, there is a psychological value in the sociability which the house-office implies.

If your objective is a post which necessitates winning city-wide or multi-neighborhood support, a centrally located headquarters is, of course, important. And it will need to be one to which party workers feel free to go at any time without fear of disturbing someone's domestic routines. In most communities there are vacant stores and offices which can be rented for reasonable sums during an election campaign. Choose one of these, decorate it suitably, and if possible hold a press conference the day it opens.

This is the appropriate point at which to state one of my own strong differences with the traditional ethos of the American political campaign. Normally very little is done by candidates and party leaders to make a campaign headquarters a pleasant and attractive place to be, except in national election contests. Local organizations are inclined to suppose that a few chairs, a couple of tables, and the inevitable battery of telephones are sufficient to make a former barbershop an adequate campaign headquarters. Consequently some of the most uncomfortable evenings of my life have been spent working in a bare, colorless, poorly heated, barnlike room with nothing but a wobbly folding chair to sit on and no sound except the rhythmic clatter of a mimeograph machine in the background.

People tolerate these conditions in the name of duty and service. But if I ever have the job of setting up a long-term headquarters and a bit of money with which to do it properly, I intend to borrow at least one leaf from the more progressive commercial institutions. I will put a bit of warmth and comfort into the place and provide radios tuned to decent music. This would not only make a more attractive setting to which to lure volunteer workers but would create, I am sure, a far more impressive image of the party in the mind of the public.

An important part of establishing a headquarters is to arrange for people to man the main telephone for up to eighteen hours a day. When one is working extensively with volunteer help, it is necessary to have an effective clearinghouse for their sporadic efforts. People who are not being paid have an understandable prejudice against having to go to great lengths to get or report back on their assignments. They want to be able to phone for instructions or for turning in their results and *find someone there.* Thus, you will need to set up four-hour shifts each day and be certain that those who sign up for them really appear.

It is equally important that those in charge of headquarters be well briefed on campaign procedures and have the telephone numbers of those to whom they can turn or refer people to for further help. The public in general (and newspaper reporters in particular) expect to get answers when they phone headquarters, not earnest ignorance.

You will be well advised, also, to have some person at headquarters at all times whose job it is to attend to the stray strangers wandering in from time to time. This is valuable from two points of view:

1. It avoids the loss of useful volunteer help which can occur when everyone ignores the quiet little man in the gray suit who stands around for thirty minutes and then leaves, taking with him a wealth of talent in organizational experience and/or a large cash contribution to a depleted war chest. Almost every campaign with which I have been associated has its story of some serious oversight of this kind.

2. The inconspicuous stranger may be an agent of the opposite party. One hapless Republican organization spent a great deal of time and worry trying to figure out how its Democratic rivals managed to become privy to its most

secret plans and never did tumble to the fact that the quiet little man in the gray suit who sat smoking in the corner evening after evening was the Democratic candidate's brother-in-law!

A well-run headquarters is invaluable as a center for the co-ordination of campaign activities and as visible evidence to the faithful that the party is in business.

Canvassing the Neighborhoods

Early in the campaign your team should begin a door-to-door canvass of the election district. These visits have several purposes:

1. They constitute a check on the voting list to be sure that those registered at an address are really resident there. When there is a discrepancy between list and residence, it should be explained and corrected or the voter should be challenged on Election Day. It is sometimes the case that people who have moved out of the district or even out of the city return there to vote in order to throw their support to friends who are running for office. This felicitous practice, although commendably loyal, should be discouraged. Especially when engaged in by the opposition party!

2. The canvasser discovers whether anyone at that address will need an absentee ballot, because of illness or intended absence from the state. Where there is such a need the fact should be reported to party headquarters and arrangements made to get an application to the person involved as quickly as possible.

3. There may be those living at the house who will need a ride to the polls on Election Day. The canvasser takes their names, finds out when they would like to be picked up, and turns the information over to the appropriate campaign official.

4. The canvasser tries as tactfully as possible to find out

anything which may help the candidate to make a personal appeal to the residents of his district. He engages the householder in conversation, if he can, about the forthcoming election and carefully notes, at first mentally and then on a card, any special concern which the voter expresses about problems or personalities. Then when the candidate himself makes his personal call or writes his personal letter he is in a position to speak to the specific interests of each constituent.

There is some difference of opinion about the degree to which the canvassing team should press for information which the householder does not volunteer freely. Some campaigners are quite aggressive in asking direct questions, including the voter's preference in the election. Others prefer a more subtle kind of canvass on the theory that too blunt an approach risks more than it gains by offending many people. My own inclination is to side with these latter. Most voters are understandably sensitive about anything that seems to them to intrude upon the secrecy of their ballot. Learning how such people intend to vote, if one does actually find out by probing, is not nearly as important as making a favorable impression on behalf of the canvasser's ticket. One of my own friends learned this lesson the hard way when, in response to persistent inquiries, a woman said angrily, "Well, O.K., if you're determined to know. I had planned to vote for your man, but now I'm not so sure!"

Before going on his rounds each canvasser should have prepared cards with data taken from the master voter list at headquarters. There should be a card for every address, showing party affiliation, if any, for each resident qualified to vote. After finishing a call the canvasser should add to the card additional information about absentee ballots, rides on Election Day, special concerns of the householder, and anything else that may be useful in the campaign.

The canvasser should also have with him a supply of the candidate's leaflets and leave one at each address on his route. As he hands the leaflet to the voter he will have an opportunity to speak his piece about the virtues of the candidate. This should be done with dignity and under no circumstances include any derogatory references to the opposition. It is my experience that this part of the call comes most appropriately at the end of the conversation. If the canvasser has handled the situation well, he will by that time have impressed himself upon the voter as a public-spirited citizen whose primary interest is in being of service to the neighborhood, and his appeal on behalf of his own candidate will be the more favorably received. Obviously this assumes a degree of personal attractiveness in the one making the canvass. But the whole idea of a canvass is based upon that assumption. People who must be known well in order to be tolerated should be put to work on less conspicuous tasks.

Where possible, of course, canvassing should be done by residents of the neighborhood. This is more likely to assure a friendly encounter and add the weight of personal influence to whatever else is accomplished by the visits. But where this cannot be arranged, the more carefully briefed each canvasser is about the make-up of the area which he is to cover the more effectively will he be able to relate to the residents. Remember, the canvasser is your personal representative. He can do you much good and a great deal of harm. See that he is well chosen and prepared.

Telephone Squads

Even the most careful canvass will leave many questions about the electorate unanswered. Thus, you must be prepared to follow up the door-to-door visits with a series of telephone calls. These will be needed in order to reach those people who were not at home when the canvass was made. (Obviously more than one visit should be planned, but often even many of them fail to reach certain residents.) The queries that would have been put face to face are made in such phone calls. In addition data about rides and absentee ballots can be double checked. The more contact you can have with the voter *without annoying him* the better your chances of winning his support. Good excuses to follow up the personal canvass with a subsequent telephone call should not be overlooked.

Perhaps the most valuable contribution of your telephone squad will be its members' calls to their friends and acquaintances. These tend to strengthen the impression that "the people whose judgment I trust are for So-and-So" and generate the very helpful feeling that there is a groundswell of enthusiasm for your candidacy. Since all of us have a more or less unrecognized wish to be on the winning side of any contest, this mood is worth encouraging.

Remember, there are many people among your volunteers whose family responsibilities or health limit the amount of door-to-door canvassing that they can do, but who will spend hours at the phone on your behalf.

Media Publicity

As indicated in an earlier chapter you must not be naïve about the way in which newspaper, radio, and television publicity is handled. When a man is famous or notorious the mass media will seek him out, and his publicity will take care of itself. But, for most of us, getting into the spotlight takes initiative and imagination. Thus, a well-run political campaign will have some one person who is designated to deal with reporters and get information to their desks.

There is neither space nor need here to detail the preparation of press releases. Anyone who has been active in community affairs long enough to run for office will have seen a great many of them. They are those mimeographed documents which often come through the mail marked "For Your Information" and "To be Released . . ." and present concise accounts of some allegedly newsworthy event. One who has *not* had access to such material will find a wealth of instruction in any newspaper story dealing with a political personality or campaign. (The chances are very good that the story is based upon and even follows the outlines of a press release prepared by one of the parties.)

There are, however, several important things to be remembered about media publicity:

1. Events make better stories than mere opinions. While you will sometimes make the news columns or broadcasts with a statement expressing an attitude toward public policy, you are more likely to do so on the basis of a "happening." Speeches made at a public meeting, proposals advanced at a legislative hearing, positions advocated during a panel discussion are of greater interest to reporters and their editors than philosophical utterances aimed at the human race from the desk in your office.

If, for example, you are outraged by the state of the streets in your community, your anger is more apt to be noted by reporters if it expresses itself in a "protest meeting" in one of the most afflicted neighborhoods. You may even get a picture in the paper or on the television, if you can be photographed pointing dramatically to a pothole while surrounded by a half dozen equally indignant citizens.

2. The events which generate good publicity are not always as spontaneous or as planned as they may appear. Let's face it. The "indignant citizens" with whom a candidate is pictured viewing the outrageous defalcations of those in power occasionally turn out to be members of the candidate's own campaign committee or relatives of the ward chairman. And, conversely, the sentiments reported as having been contained in a "speech" may actually have been uttered rather casually between bites of a sandwich at an envelope-stuffing session of the Volunteers for You.

A good publicity chairman can build appealing stories out of fairly meager sources. On one occasion in my own campaigning I was astounded to read in the morning paper that I had dealt at length with several crucial issues in a speech on the previous evening. The truth was that I had failed rather dismally to say anything relevant on that occasion, and my trustworthy volunteers had been forced to fill in as best they could!

Obviously the best campaign is one which sets up authentic occasions for publicity releases. But the newcomer to political office-seeking should not be too legalistic in his definition of newsworthy "events."

3. Get your material to the offices of the newspaper, radio station, and television studio in plenty of time to make the press or script deadline. Do not be embarrassed about taking the release to the office yourself. Reporters are used to this and appreciate the co-operation. They need material for their columns and broadcasts and are happy to get it without too much running around from place to place.

4. Remember that human interest factors make the best stories even better. Adlai Stevenson rising to make a major address with a hole in the sole of his shoe, John F. Ken-

nedy having to put his son on someone's lap before being able to go on with his speech, and Dwight Eisenhower's annoyance at a slow teleprompter all got more publicity than the words which followed.

The same is true at the local political level. When the community's oldest Democrat announces that he will vote Republican for the first time in his life or the candidate's mother agrees to reveal the secret of her fabulous plum pudding to anyone who agrees to contribute to her son's war chest, the ears of the reporters will probably be open and their pens prepared.

5. Be sure that your press releases contain "quotable quotes." Direct quotations that can be attributed safely to the candidate make a news story far more attractive to the media than general statements to the effect that the candidate "said that . . . such and such is the case."

There is an important warning to be offered about media publicity. You should resist the temptation to allow the substance of your campaign to be determined by the desire for attention in the newspapers and on the air. Well-meaning friends will encourage you to stress this or that because it has media appeal. Reporters themselves may on occasion try to get you to say something which you do not really believe in order to supply them with a dramatic headline or lead sentence. This kind of thing is tempting. But it gets to be a bad habit and can take your campaign emphasis far from where you want it. Make your campaign newsworthy. But keep it *your* campaign.

Fund Raising

If your campaign is one which aims at election to major office, fund-raising will have to be turned over to those who make a career of it. Sometimes this means a nonpolitical public relations firm, at other times a party official who is assigned the responsibility on a long-term basis. Here, again, any effort to suggest procedures in a book such as this would be an exercise in futility.

But if you are aiming at a more humble political post, and your anticipated expenditures will run somewhere between $500 and $1,000, you will in all probability have to carry some share of the financial burden yourself and also assist in the solicitation of contributions from others. For such a campaign there are a few helpful generalizations that can be offered here:

1. Expect to put out a good part of the cost of campaigning from your own pocket. Political parties differ from place to place in what a local candidate can expect from the central organization. But it rarely amounts to a great deal. The assumption is generally made that the publicity that is given to the party's headliners, *i.e.,* candidates for the big jobs, will rub off on the coat-tail riders. And this is often all that you can anticipate receiving from "downtown."

There are exceptions, of course. If the contest in your district has special meaning because of local issues or personality conflicts, you may find the organization somewhat more generous. And once you are established in office and have turned out to be a credit to your colleagues in high places, you have a right to expect assistance, particularly if you seem to be facing a tough re-election race. (It can make one feel "knighted" to receive a phone call from the Town Chairman offering financial aid in this miniature crusade!)

2. The best technique for money raising is that which promises the most return for the least outlay. This may seem so obvious as to need no elaboration. But one who has been active in politics for any period of time will be familiar with the elaborate money-raising affairs, *i.e.,* dinners, clambakes, slick promotional drives, etc., which end

up handling a great deal of cash and hanging on to very little of it for campaign purposes. Personal contact by volunteers with their friends and neighbors is probably the best device in local campaigning. It is not too difficult to ask and receive $5 and $10 contributions toward the election of an able man or woman. If your reputation is solid and your record of public service a good one, you will be able to pay many of your bills with such small donations. And the overhead involved in their collection is negligible.

3. Go after a few major contributors yourself. And remember that you do have a claim on this kind of support. Unless the position for which you are running pays a large salary (and this is rarely the case at the local level), you are giving far more to the service of the community than most of your neighbors. This does not mean that you can be either arrogant or confident about soliciting financial aid. But it does mean that you need not be hesitant about doing so.

4. While it is unwise to overburden those who are giving time and personal effort on your behalf, do not hesitate to seek financial support from those volunteers who are giving other forms of assistance. These are the people who will have developed a psychological vested interest in your victory and are in the best position to see just how badly money is needed if the campaign is to be carried forward successfully. Give them a chance to add dollars to their enthusiasm.

Your Personal Campaign

No matter how well organized and enthusiastic your party staff and their volunteer helpers are the real drive wheel of your organization will be what is called your "personal campaign." This means the complex of individual contacts which only you can make. There is something almost mystical in the faith which experienced politicians invest in this aspect of their careers. And it is often moving to see the hope which your most sophisticated supporters build around this center of your common effort. You will be asked again and again in the early days of the contest, "And how is your personal campaign going." And when you begin to hear others refer to the vigor and effectiveness of that personal campaign, you will feel a genuine thrill of satisfaction.

Let's look at some of the elements in this critical phase of democratic politicking:

"Hit Every Doorbell"

Everyone to whom I turned for advice in my first campaign stressed that tactic. If I heard it once during September of 1963, I heard it at least fifty times. Hit every doorbell. Keep going back until you have talked with each voter or at any rate a member of his family. I must admit that I listened to these counsels with a good deal of skepticism. I had never been visited by a candidate for office and doubted that such a call would have influenced my vote in an election of any importance. The idea of trudging through the fading light of an October afternoon with an armload of pamphlets terrified me. But the impact of repetition was impossible to ignore. So I did indeed hit every doorbell. And it worked.

Now when I say that it worked I am not attributing my election to that tactic alone or even chiefly. What I mean is that the effect of those calls on voters had a profound effect on me. Far from being hostile or indifferent I found that most of the people in the 18th Ward were both cordial and interested. Like me, they had never been called upon by a candidate before. Some were flattered, some amused, and a few grateful for the opportunity to raise local issues that had been bothering them. Almost without exception they were courteous, even gracious, in their reception of me.

This process of hitting every doorbell brought me to life as a candidate, gave me the drive to organize a sustained campaign by my volunteers, and earned me the vigorous support of party regulars. There is nothing as likely to send you out again and again into the autumnal rains with your packet of damp pamphlets as the word filtering back from "downtown" that you are running "one helluva good campaign out there." And this same inspiring experience can give you the brass to play the game like a pro.

The business of personal calls is really very simple once you get over the initial nervousness. Clutch your leaflet in one hot fist and begin knocking on doors with the other. The first door is the hardest. Once you have opened that one the whole process becomes simpler and eventually good fun.

Here are a few tips to help with these calls:

1. Pick a time of day at which you can be reasonably sure of finding your voters at home and not deeply enmeshed in dinner or some other family enterprise. These periods will differ from block to block depending upon sociological factors. Men who work in factories tend to want their dinners earlier than those who come home from professional offices. If you move quickly, you may be able to hit these factory workers between the time they walk in at the front door and the time dinner is served. You can get some clues here by watching the automobiles arriving or already parked in the driveways. (I felt a hood on occasion to determine whether a car had just been parked or had been there all day.)

You will make a good many miscalculations at this point. When you find that you have in fact interrupted someone's dinner, apologize, hand the householder a pamphlet and beat a hasty retreat. *Then,* drop him a note by mail that evening repeating your regret and making a brief pitch for his support. Not all those whom you interrupt will let you leave. Some are almost apologetic about being in the midst of a meal and will give you an opportunity to make your full spiel. (A few will even invite you to have a cup of coffee and some dessert!) These, too, are naturals for a follow-up letter expressing special appreciation on your part.

2. Treat the whole process with a bit of humor. Make it clear that you realize this is a political ritual more joked about than practiced, but that you are finding it a rewarding and enlightening experience. If you seem a bit apologetic about the intrusion, the voter will often end up encouraging you to keep up the good work and assure you of his family's support.

3. Keep your pitch short. Introduce yourself, tell why you are there, ask the voter's name, and in two or three sentences give your most relevant reason (in that neighborhood) for being a candidate. Then offer to answer any questions he may have about local problems or election procedures, ask if anyone needs an absentee ballot or a ride to the polls, and point out on your leaflet the telephone number, where he can get further information.

If you have done your homework prior to starting out on your calls, you will, of course, know whether there is anything about this voter in the way of special concerns, friends in common, prominence in some neighborhood activity, etc., to which you can helpfully refer in your remarks. Do not miss the chance for such individual touches. You will be surprised at how even a little bit of special attention will bring a very cordial response.

4. Avoid settling down in someone's living room. You may end up spending far more time there than you can

afford. If the weather makes it wise to step inside, stay near the door and make it clear that you have many calls to make and are determined not to trespass on anyone's hospitality.

5. After each visit make a note about the nature of the encounter. This will come in handy when you wish to follow up the personal canvass with letters or telephone calls. Be sure to include any unusual aspect of the visit, *e.g.,* the dog that took to you or almost bit you, the offer of dessert, the discovery of a mutual friend, anything that you may want to refer to in future relationships with the voter. And if there is something about him that will enable you to remember his face and greet him by name when he comes into the polls on Election Day, by all means make the effort to do so.

Your Telephone Follow-up

When the hour or the weather makes it impossible to do any further doorbell ringing on a given day, you are ready to sit down for a spell of telephone calls. If *anything* occurred during one of your visits that gives you an excuse to telephone the voter, by all means consider doing it. Confirm some bit of information that was asked for. Report that you have arranged the absentee ballot application or Election Day ride to the polls. Express regret that only one member of the family was in when you called and inquire whether the others have questions.

Now obviously you will not have time to reach very many of your constituents in this way. But if you phone a select list in each neighborhood, the word will get around that you are an aggressive campaigner with a real interest in the voter. And this always seems, for some reason which eludes me, to boost your stock greatly.

Personal Letters

When the evening is far spent and your finger is worn
our from dialing the telephone, you may begin writing
short personal letters. Some of these notes will go to people
whom you have not been able to find at home in your canvass of the neighborhoods. Others will take the place of a
phone call in confirming some arrangement or information
given. Occasionally such epistles will be your only contact
with the rare voter who should not be visited personally,
e.g., the man who is known to loathe politicians, the family
recently bereaved, or the elderly woman who lives on the
third floor of a walk-up and must trudge down three flights
of stairs to answer the door.

Whatever their ostensible purpose these letters should
bear your personal cachet. If your script is legible, write
longhand. If you have a battered typewriter which be-
speaks your own erratic touch, use it. I well remember the
sophisticated young matron who almost voted for my opponent, because he had written "a note in his own hand,
and with a ball-point pen."

Campaign Oratory

One of the surprises in store for the newcomer to politics is the relatively small part played in local campaigns
by speechmaking. The fact is that most candidates for
office rarely, if ever, address more than a dozen people at
one time. And such occasions are so informal in character
that what is said hardly qualifies as a speech. You have to
get up to the level of the "city ticket" (that is, run for a
city-wide post) before the chance to harangue the multitude comes along. For the most part the candidate for the
School Board, the Town Council, or the post of Second
Selectman is seen more than he is heard and does most of
his talking to individuals.

The hard truth is that people are no longer interested in hearing political speeches, except when they are delivered by distinguished men who are battling for major offices. Even then they expect to have those philippics presented to them on television, so that they can get the drama of the event with commentary and without moving from their armchairs. The massed faces which one sees at the rallies staged for Presidential candidates are made up for the most part of loyal organization men and women and their families who have been dragooned into showing up in order to make the occasion seem to be what it is not. And no one is going to expend the effort needed to turn out a crowd for even the most inspiring candidate for alderman!

As a quite practical matter many of the smaller electoral districts do not even contain a hall suitable for a large public meeting. When we prepared to have a "Candidates Reception" in my New Haven ward, we found that there was no room inside the boundaries of the ward big enough to hold even the modest throng anticipated. Sometimes a church will grant the use of its basement, and some school authorities allow their auditoriums to be rented out to political gatherings. But frequently the largest room in the community is some private home's recreation area.

From time to time, however, you may find yourself given the chance to make a campaign speech, so here are a few suggestions:

1. Make it constructive. Unless the audience is composed entirely of your partisans who have gathered to hear you "lay it on" the opposition, the more you concentrate on constructive proposals the better.

2. Remember that the first purpose of every political speech is to win support for your candidacy. *What* you say is secondary to the *way* in which you say it. This is not cynicism. It is simply an honest recognition of the objective of political oratory. If people want to hear a lecture

on economics or education, they will go to an authority on the subject. When they listen to a politician, they are trying to get a fix on his personal ability to understand and deal with the political aspects of the problem.

I am not suggesting that you lie or distort your views for effect. What I *am* proposing is that you select the amount of material to be covered and the organization of the speech in such a way as to allow *you* to do a competent job. It is not uncommon to hear very able men put their worst foot forward trying to cover too much ground in a didactic essay disguised as a speech. They inform no one and impress the audience only with their fumbling incompetence. Keep your speech simple. A few significant points well illustrated and backed up by clearly presented evidence. Such a basic structure will give an opportunity for you to display whatever rhetorical gifts you possess but will not make unreasonable demands upon you.

3. Allow an opportunity for questions after your speech. Be sure to plant some good ones to get things started and also permit you to speak a few impressive words on crucial issues.

4. You need not pretend to know everything there is to be known about every topic. Audiences are not dismayed by a man who honestly admits there are problems to which he needs to give further study. This kind of candor should be cultivated. It will keep you from many uncomfortable spots and turn limitations into assets.

5. Unless you are engaged in a bloody war within the party, be sure to say a few kind words about those running with you on the ticket. This is one of the standard courtesies of political life, and it is amazing how many hardbitten old professionals will be delighted by such praise or offended by its absence.

Walking Your Beat on Election Day

On the last evening of my first campaign I collapsed. Literally. Two months of tremendous effort caught up with me as I was talking to a small group of teachers and students at a local girls college. In the middle of my speech I had to ask to be excused and was driven home. I was violently nauseated, dizzy, and suffering from a severe headache. The campaign had ended, and so, it seemed, had I.

But early the next morning (Election Day), I was on the corner near the polling place greeting the first voters arriving to cast their ballots. That particular day is a hazy memory, but I have walked the same beat many times since. And it pays.

As indicated earlier in this chapter the primary value of your presence on that windy street corner is its effect on the morale of those who are bringing in the voters. Their efforts are crucial to your success. Many elections are won or lost on the basis of who gets out the vote. And the vote will be gotten out in proportion to the enthusiasm of those who are working. When the drivers and canvassers see you come up to their cars to greet the people they have brought in, they cannot help feeling an obligation to match your efforts right down the line. The candidate who has played out this ritual of politicking is the one whose workers are still going strong, fighting to get out those last few tardy voters when the polling place finally closes.

And beyond its influence upon your workers the beat walking routine does make a few last-minute converts. Especially if you organize it properly. Here's an important tip:

Whenever one of your cars goes out to pick up a voter have the driver print the name of his passenger in large block letters on a card and fasten it to the outside of one of the sun visors, so that only you can see it. Then, as you approach the car to welcome the voter to the polls, you can call him or her by name. If necessary the driver can even add the street from which the people come. Thus, you will be able to make some appropriate reference about being happy to see Such-and-Such Avenue so well represented. These pleasantries can and sometimes do make a last-minute difference in the minds of voters.

Needless to say, you observe carefully the official boundaries beyond which you may not carry your campaign toward the polling place. And it is my own considered opinion that the softer the sell at this point the better. You are out there to greet the residents of the neighborhood as they participate in the primary duty of citizenship. That should be the aura surrounding your presence and the guide to whatever you actually say to them. Your opponent will probably be there, too. Do not be alarmed if he seems to know far more people than you do. He is feeling the same way about you!

Postscript

One last bit of advice. If you have an interest in politics, marry a girl who shares that interest and has a strong success orientation. My wife Ruth was the dynamo of my campaign organization. She did more work than the rest of us put together. And when a friend congratulated her on her "wifely devotion" to my political career, Ruth responded, "Wifely devotion, hell! I'm just a rotten loser."

That's the spirit that wins elections.

7

The New Politics

In the spring of 1968 Joseph Duffy, national chairman of Americans for Democratic Action and later a reform Democratic candidate for election to the United States Senate, gave a talk at Yale University on "The New Politics." When he had finished, a member of the faculty commented, "Well, Joe, your 'new politics' sounds to me very much like the old politics with some new men running the machine." The reaction of the audience was a burst of laughter and applause. And Duffy himself wryly acknowledge that it was a lot easier to make the distinction in theory than in practice. When organizing for action, he confessed, you learn that there is more to be said for traditional procedures than might have been supposed.

This is a discovery that a great many people, especially young men and women, are making in the present period. The methods of political action that have evolved in the United States over the past one hundred years represent something more than mere social accident or the convenience of professional politicians. They are by no means perfect implementations of ideal democracy, and they need constant reforming. But they have been hammered out through decades of hard experience. And their faults, while

139

serious, reflect as much upon our people and social institutions generally as they do upon the political system itself.
Many of what appear to be unwise or even undemocratic
practices turn out upon closer examination to be accommodations to eccentricities in the national character or
efforts to cope with the determined political irresponsibility of the mass of Americans. Among the throngs of
unsung heroes who fade into the nation's past in every
generation are a great many "politicians" who, sometimes
by means that they could not defend in public, have built
a viable democracy from very fragile materials.

No appreciation of the past, however, can blind us to
the importance of change in the operation of our political
system. Indeed, the persistent demand for reform constitutes one of the most significant dynamics in the successful
operation of our kind of party government.

If the average American can be said to have any conviction about the political process, it is probably the certainty that the whole business can stand a good shake-up
and some drastic improving. Justified or not in any given
historical period, this idea serves to keep our politics relatively open-ended and creates an atmosphere in which
new segments of the population are admitted to the centers of decision-making and enabled to stamp something
of their character upon the outline of the national future.
The popular disposition to "throw the rascals out" as a
solution to social problems leaves much to be desired in
terms of both rationality and justice. But as a practical
matter it has made American politics among the most responsibly flexible in the world.

But it is not always easy to define and discuss the
changes that keep occurring in our system, as Mr. Duffy
pointed out. This is true precisely because of the pervasiveness of change combined with the nonideological and personality-oriented nature of our political process. In some

countries which operate on a multiple-party basis each party represents a rather well-worked-out ideological position or social philosophy. Thus, when one Administration is removed from office and another takes its place the policy implications are clear and dramatic. Social legislation, tax programs, international relations and every other aspect of the nation's political life undergo abrupt and sweeping alterations that only the most obtuse can ignore. In the United States, however, the fact that our two-party system is organized around personalities more than principles and directs its energies toward gaining and keeping power rather than promoting a detailed program makes the process of change much more subtle and the accomplished fact quite evasive.

This aspect of our tradition is nowhere more vividly illustrated than in the Administrations of Franklin D. Roosevelt. During the 1930's the Government of the United States altered course on critical policy matters more often than one of the President's beloved sailboats! Tight money and loose spending, protection and free trade, controlled monopoly and enforced competition, isolation and internationalism replaced each other from month to month to the dismay of ideologues and the delight of a pragmatic public. The personalities of a few men, headed by the charismatic Roosevelt, were about the only thread that tied together the fabric of the New Deal. And the people loved it!

It is easy to attribute this course of events to some instability in the temperament of the President and his advisers. And this was done loudly by leading Republicans. But the truth is that in the face of a national economic disaster and a foreign scene fraught with increasing peril Mr. Roosevelt was using the flexibility of our political system to feel his way through the darkness of unprecedented crises. While France was enduring a succession of regimes, with the attendant intensification of her suffering, the United States was experimenting with a diversity of policies while enjoying the benefits of continuity in administration.

The same sort of thing happened in less obvious ways during the Presidencies of Harry Truman, Dwight Eisenhower, and John F. Kennedy. And the record of the Nixon Administration makes it clear that the American political ethos has not altered in this respect. We continue to make our significant policy changes as much *within* Administrations as between them. This process has been called the genius of the two-party system, since it avoids radical polarization of the populace along partisan lines and charges each of the major parties with tasks of interpretation and reconciliation as well as opposition.

In spite of the subtlety with which political change tends to occur in the United States there are in every generation some trends which can be discerned and which give their special flavor to the time. One of the most significant of these today is known, for want of a more precise name, as "the new politics." It embraces a variety of diverse personalities from the roster of traditional politicians, and has its supportive factions in both the liberal and conservative camps of the major parties. Those who have studied the new politics in operation agree that its primary characteristic is the effort to involve more people in the process of making political decisions. This attempt operates at two levels:

First, the new politicians have less confidence in the omniscience of government, especially Federal Government, than their liberal friends and have more faith in the wisdom of the people than do orthodox conservatives.

It is unfair to allege, as many do today, that the knee-jerk response of traditional liberals to any social problem was to propose that it be turned over for solution to some governmental agency with power and expertise. But there is certainly an element of truth in that charge. The pervasive leadership qualities of President Roosevelt continued to cast a glow of omnicompetence around the principle of government management long after Roosevelt had died. This mood was, of course, reinforced by the necessities of World War II which led to the centralization of power in many areas of our national life and the delegation of previously private authority to political management.

Today even the most ardent disciples of the original New Dealers have begun to recognize the limitations of governmental competence. And the new politicians have made a principle of this disenchantment. They point to massive Federal programs in the field of urban renewal, for example, which have imposed drastic solutions upon communities blighted by economic decay. And they argue, with much justification, that the people most affected by such programs have had too little voice in their formulation. In many cases low-rent housing has been torn down to make room for expensive high-rise apartments and whole residential areas have been replaced by commercial buildings with no provision being made for those left homeless by the change. Superhighways increasingly determine the shape of the community, while the community itself has almost nothing to say about the location of such highways.

For the most part the conflict between the traditional government planners and the new politicians is not one which centers in ultimate objectives. Both want prosperous citizens, a healthy economy, and humane communities. Their difference is over the correct order of priorities and the way in which those priorities are to be set. This is a more significant distinction, however, than may seem at first glance, and it will pay us to give it some attention here.

The orthodox approach to community renewal begins with the rehabilitation of urban commercial centers. Its fundamental assumption is that there can be no permanent improvement in the welfare of human beings until the economy of their region has been put upon a sound basis. There is no point, the supporters of this position argue, in building low-cost housing, parks, and cultural facilities, if people have no jobs. Even the least expensive home is too costly for the unemployed, and parks and cultural centers are perverted from their real purpose if they deteriorate into refuges for those who cannot find work. Revitalize the economic center of the community, they insist, and the impetus to further and more clearly humane improvements will be almost self-generating. Men with jobs and money will create a healthy demand for housing and the other amenities of life.

Those who adopt such a line are not naïve enough to believe that the process will be quite so simple. To do them justice one must point out that they divide into at least two camps. Those who believe that the second part of the process (*i.e.,* the growth of more humane cities) will occur naturally as a result of the dynamics of free enterprise, and those who are prepared to guarantee that it will take place by massive programs of governmental subsidies in the fields of housing, education, recreation, and so on. Whole volumes have been written on the importance of the difference between these positions. But for our purposes here they may be lumped together because of their primary emphasis upon commercial renewal as the basis for a healthy community.

The new politics challenges this basic assumption. Its disciples contend that the shape of the community ought not be determined by the needs of commerce, that the development of economic institutions should follow lines laid down by the human values to which the people are committed. It is wrong, they argue, to subordinate neighborhood and family patterns to the requirements of commercial success—to lay out a city, for example, to suit the convenience of businessmen and then allow or compel the human beings to fit themselves into the cracks, as it were, or around the edges. Commerce is adaptable. It does not have to be given ideal conditions in order to develop and flourish. It can and should mould itself around the structures established by our vision of the good life and the humane community.

Since the new politics puts so much stress upon the building of *humanly* rather than *commercially* oriented structures and processes, it follows inevitably that its disciples reject programs imposed from the top, especially those which accept the primacy of commercial renewal as their starting point. New politicians want redevelopment plans to originate with the people who live in the area affected and be subject at every critical point to their judgment. There is, of course, a great diversity of opinion among the new politicians about the techniques by which these objectives are to be reached. The right wing of the new politics would like to see such judgments expressed through the traditional structures and "natural" leaders of the locality, while the left wing favors pure democracy and such new procedures as may be necessary to effectuate it. On the desirability of local control, however, they are in agreement.

This position has tremendous appeal for anyone who feels troubled by the ascendancy of commercialism in American life, and who chafes at the punch-card mentality so characteristic of highly centralized governmental agencies. To spend an evening watching television and the efforts of business enterprise to induce hypnotic acquiescence in consumers can be a dismaying experience, even more dismaying than trying to fight one's way through the forms and questionnaires emanating from political bureaucracies. One is strongly tempted to proclaim the new politics as the prophetic movement of our time.

There are, however, three important problems faced by the new politician which cannot be wished out of existence by even the most heated indignation against present iniquities:

1. The idea that "the business of America is business," as a President of the United States once put it, cannot be easily changed. The effort to return commerce to its proper place (*i.e.,* that of servant of the community's human concerns) will not meet with immediate acceptance and success, even though one can quote Adam Smith, David Ricardo, and a host of free-enterprise economists on its behalf. The community which attempts to push commerce from center stage and give a more prominent place to the human image finds itself threatened with wholesale abandonment by the enterprises on which it *must* depend to some degree for its survival. Cities which enforce their antipollution ordinances or reserve the most desirable land sites for houses and schools are constantly in danger of seeing factories move to less progressive locations.

This is the paradox which the new politics confronted early in the game. The local autonomy for which it fights is in a sense its Achilles heel. Where renewal and planning goals are set by some central authority the efforts of business to play one community against another are useless, since the same rules and standards obtain wherever an enterprise might go. In the absence of such central authority, however, these same efforts have proven highly effective. Thus, a critical question for the advocate of community control is: How can local autonomy cope with inter-

state commerce? Unless it finds some new formula for doing so, the struggle of the new politics to reverse the relationship of economic to social values is doomed at the
outset.

2. The job of getting the people of a neighborhood to
attend a series of meetings and give serious thought to the
problems of their community is an extremely difficult one.
This fact is often lost sight of because of the ease with
which masses of indignant citizens can be turned out for
one or two sessions in protest against something that they
do *not* want. There is a world of difference, however,
between such one-shot rallies based upon instant indignation and the long tedious business of planning for the future of a complex social organization. Men and women
who work all day at jobs of their own and recognize that
they have no special training for city planning quickly
grow bored when confronted by elaborate charts, blue
prints, and sheets of statistical data. This is perfectly understandable.

It should be equally understandable, then, that what
almost invariably occurs is that a fraction of the community sticks at the job and makes the final decisions or else
the whole task is delegated to a staff of professionals who
may be even less sensitive and accountable to the neighborhood than the much maligned bureaucrat. In short, insistence upon pure democracy frequently leads to its exact
opposite. Where authority is admittedly being exercised by
representatives on behalf of the people, there are normally
provisions by which such authorities are kept accountable
to those whom they represent. But where the people are
ostensibly acting as a committee of the whole, no such
precautions are thought necessary and the result is often
the tyranny of an articulate minority from whose decisions
there is no appeal.

3. The new politician is in danger of romanticizing "the

people" as many reformers before him have done. He is tempted to suppose that grass-roots organizations will, by their very nature, be more community conscious and less dominated by special interest than are state and Federal Government agencies. In a sense, of course, this assumption is correct. It is a great deal more difficult for traditional lobbyists and their clients to "get to" a host of neighborhood groups and control their decisions than it is to reach some vulnerable individual or staff in one central location. One of the more petulant Roman emperors wished fervently that his subjects had but a single head so that he could cut it off with one stroke. This has been a dream of tyrants through the ages. And it symbolizes the advantage to democracy of dispersed decision-making power.

It would be a mistake, however, to think that because they do not have dramatic corporate identities and headquarters in some large city special interests do not exist and do their self-serving work in neighborhood organizations. Every community is in a sense a microcosm of the nation. Even when it is homogeneous in economic, ethnic, and other social terms, it is divided into a great variety of factions and alliances, each of which serves a purpose as dear to individual hearts and egos as any land acquisition project or traction franchise to a business combine. The people who live at one end of a given city block or rural township will polarize as bitterly over a traffic light at the corner or the location of a school-bus stop as will members of the United Nations debating matters of international policy. In fact, it has been my own experience that there is often more passion and less reason in such discussions than one finds in even the most "interest"-dominated legislative body. Being few in number and residing in a small area does not prevent men and women from asserting their own special concerns in violent and uncompromising fashion.

It is important, therefore, to remember that the strength of democracy lies not in some doctrine of popular virtue but in the checking and balancing function that takes place when a variety of interests are forced to meet and reconcile themselves to one another. Any approach to community organization which does not take account of this ineradicable fact of life is going to face certain defeat.

These are the three serious problems that face the proponents of the new politics (the politics of participation): the traditional primacy of economic values over social objectives which has characterized American history, the unwillingness of masses of men and women to engage in arduous decision-making for which they feel ill-equipped, and the special interests which exist in and divide even the most monolithic community structure.

Do these problems mean that the new politics is doomed to fail in its efforts to make our social order more humane? Not necessarily. For the new politicians, as their name implies, have a second level of concern, another area in which they are working to realize their objective. And that is the democratization of our political parties themselves. The new politicians argue, quite correctly, that one can be a lifelong registered Republican or Democrat without ever having an opportunity to contribute to the governance of his party. It is their contention that politics must be taken out of the proverbial "smoke-filled room" and turned over to the citizens of the community. Now, of course, there is nothing particularly new about this proposal when it is stated as a pious generalization. The constant cry of those out of power and eager to get back into power is that they have been made the victims of secret deals and closed-door decisions. At the very moment this is being written,

disappointed candidates for positions on Republican and
Democratic state tickets in various parts of the country are
filling the air with charges that their successful competi-
tors were hand-picked by the bosses and forced upon reluctant conventions by coercive methods. Many of these
losers are demanding that the whole convention system be
scrapped and replaced by the direct primary.

What is *new* about the new politics position in this regard is the emphasis upon working at the neighborhood
level both to produce the desired change and to make it
effective once achieved. In contrast with orthodox practitioners the new politicians do not want to take over a few
leadership positions and leave the basic organization in-
tact. In a sense they are out to destroy "the organization"
(using that phrase to mean the small group of people who,
because of the default of most voters, have been allowed
and even forced to wield the power of party functions).
They seek to establish a kind of political process in which
day-to-day participation by most citizens will become a
reality and the old annual or biennial liturgy a thing of the
past.

This ambition relates quite logically to the other facet
of the new politics—*i.e.,* the effort to return the decision-
making process to the neighborhood level. When one really
believes that policy should be formulated by those most
immediately affected by it, one does not fear to awaken
the political consciousness and organize the human re-
sources of the community. We saw earlier that the orthodox politician is handicapped in his crusade by the self-
imposed rule against "stirring things up," that he wants to
keep politics a realm of limited warfare in which no one
endangers the traditional way of operating by raising in-
flammatory issues and thus encouraging broad-based organization. But it is precisely these two things that the new
politician seeks to realize: issue orientation and mass par-

ticipation. Because he wants, passionately in most cases, to see these same elements injected into the governmental process itself. Thus, he does not suffer from the divided mind which characterizes his more orthodox colleagues.

The attempt to democratize the major parties faces serious problems, of course. Some of these problems are the very ones which confront efforts to decentralize governmental functions. But the most serious of these is avoided —*i.e.,* the job of getting and keeping large numbers of laymen interested in what are often highly technical planning decisions. For the democratization of party organizations does not necessarily abrogate the delegation of power and responsibility to the administration elected by the voters. Partisan political involvement is not always fascinating. Indeed, it can be as boring as blueprints. But it does not assume skills which the participant does not possess, nor does it ask him to accept responsibility for programs which he has too little time and energy to study carefully.

The willingness of the new politician to see the functions of government returned to the nation's communities makes him willing to work vigorously for the increase of popular participation in politics. But it does not necessarily follow that this second objective, if achieved, will make the first feasible. Be that as it may, these two aims can be separated, and the effort to make political parties more truly instrumentalities of the popular will does not depend for its success upon turning all of us into effective planning administrators.

It is important to note here that the emphasis of the new politics upon neighborhood organization has been both stimulated and facilitated by the rapid development of this stance in the black communities of the United States. Black Americans who were once voted by the machines, like other ethnic groups before them, have begun to break that pattern. Unlike many other minorities, however, they are tending to resist full assimilation into existing power structures and are working instead to build a black-power base from which to bargain for legitimate ends of their own. Since our black citizens have been forced to live in segregated neighborhoods, the drive toward black self-assertion has become almost automatically a demand for greater local autonomy. And this fact has given an impetus to the movement which it might otherwise have lacked.

While the example of black power has had value for the new politics, however, it also points dramatically to one of the serious difficulties. How will the new politics cope with the divisive effects of ethnic loyalties upon the formulation of issue-oriented party programs? The traditional politician deals with the differences among nationality and racial factions in the community by avoiding discussion of the issues which raise and intensify intergroup antagonisms. He attempts to acknowledge the various ethnic backgrounds represented in his constituency by offering the voters a "balanced" ticket. That is to say, the party nominates for office a slate of candidates on which all of the significant social elements of the electoral district are represented. These men then use their personal contacts among their ethnic fellows in order to solicit support for the whole ticket. Sometimes they discuss policy questions which are of particular importance to that segment of the community and can be counted upon to present the party's position in the most favorable way. At other times they merely socialize at lodge meetings, picnics, and such events and allow the voter to assume that his ethnic interests will be well cared for by a so obviously loyal member of the family.

It would not be wise to stress too greatly the influence of such group loyalties upon national elections and upon the decisions of the national-party policymakers. When one takes the country as a whole a variety of considerations comes into play which minimizes these relatively parochial interests. But it is of the essence of the new politics that it seeks to build upon a neighborhood base and to involve the men and women of local communities in a new issue-oriented party organization. How to do this without exacerbating a multitude of intergroup antagonisms which traditional politics has papered over is a problem of major proportions. Quite clearly it must be done, if there is to be any rationality injected into the operation of the major parties at the local level. But the task will involve a high degree of both dedication and ingenuity.

One thing is certain. The new politics cannot afford to neglect the "social" function which politics has traditionally played in the life of the American community. The sophisticated may laugh at the clambake and the party picnic, at the campaign rally and the post-election celebration. But they do so at their peril. These are important occasions for those who devote themselves to politics. And they will become increasingly important as issue concerns are injected into party activity at the grass-roots level. For it is at such events that people come together as Republicans and Democrats primarily and subordinate for a time the ethnic, economic, and ideological quarrels which divide them. Far from making such socializing occasions less significant, the emphasis of the new politics on substantive programs increases their usefulness.

This last may seem a trivial point to one inexperienced in grass-roots politics. But those who have seen thorny questions settled over a rare steak or even some creamed chicken will not underestimate its importance. Indeed, if I were asked to list the dangers which face the new politicians as they go about their work of rebuilding our parties in more democratic forms, the first on the list would be the possibility that in their preoccupation with issues the practitioners of the new politics will fail to take adequate account of the personal relationships and loyalties which are essential to party structure. When issue divides, affection can often reunite. The wounds opened in debate are most often healed by the balm of good fellowship!

The future of the new politics can be summed up in the following way:

The dream of a decentralized American society in which the functions of government are dispersed among the multitudinous communities which make up the nation and in which the people of individual neighborhoods plan their own future in detail seems destined to go unfulfilled. More factors than can be enumerated here are driving the United States, along with all other countries in the world, toward an ever-increasing centralization of authority. We have learned that big business has much to offer the consumer in benefits which its smaller counterparts cannot yield. And experience has taught us that big business can only be regulated by governmental units with comparable spheres of authority. If Americans were willing to give up the advantages of corporate size and settle for more intimate commercial and political arrangements, the dream of a Jeffersonian form of democracy might be realized. But in the face of the public's massive acceptance of impersonal efficiency it seems clearly quixotic to hope for such a change in the national momentum.

It is not even clear, moreover, that decentralization of government *would* increase the humanity of our social order. As a number of modern political commentators have pointed out, the equation of localism with humane freedom is more logical than proven by experience. It is *local* school boards that fire controversial teachers and ban "subversive" books from library shelves. And it is the Supreme Court in faraway Washington which reverses such acts. The Congress of the United States enacts legislation intended to equalize educational opportunities and bar racial discrimination, while state and city governments often throw every possible roadblock in the way of these programs. Civil servants at the county courthouse are often exploited and shamelessly used by special interests. Employees of the Federal Government have the protection of elaborate review procedures when subjected to unjust accusation. All this is not to argue that community self-determination has no place in the American future. It is merely to point out that the case which equates local control with liberal humanitarianism is by no means onesided. There is as much evidence to suggest the opposite correlation.

Many of the experiments in neighborhood planning now being carried on will be of great value to the future of democracy in our country. They have given government officials in the state and national capitals new insights into the needs and desires of their constituents. And they, and their successor programs, can continue to do this effectively in the years ahead. But it seems clear that their role will be largely advisory, that specific questions of values and goals will be asked of them rather than carte blanche discretion given them to originate and administer complex projects on their own terms.

This does not mean that local proposals will be *merely* advisory and thus easy to be ignored by central government agencies. We have learned from the politics of confrontation in recent years that where a community organization feels strongly about some use or abuse of power it can rally impressive support for its position and make that support effective as a political weapon. The fact that community self-planning as visualized by some of its more ardent supporters will probably give way before the push toward centralized policymaking by no means implies that the energies and concerns generated by that vision will cease to have impact upon the shape of things to come.

Precisely because the first half of the new politicians' dream is unlikely to materialize, the second part becomes of tremendous importance and achieves dramatic impetus toward realization. If *governmental* power is, as seems likely, going to increase and become more and more highly centralized in its official forms, the democratization of the major parties with an accompanying increase of popular participation in their decision-making takes on added significance and feasibility.

For, the more powerful government becomes, the greater the need for effective control over that power. And the easier it is to demonstrate to the electorate both the truth and importance of that fact. Americans have shirked their political responsibilities over the years because they have not taken the national state seriously. It has been a vague and remote entity hovering in the background of national consciousness, making occasional dramatic demands in times of crisis, but never a real force in the daily life of the individual. The *idea* of government has always been suspect in our culture. But the *fact* has been little understood. And in consequence Americans have regarded politics as a peripheral activity.

It is true, of course, that during the past half century the role of government in the United States has been steadily expanding. This is attested to by the agonized curses of those who have felt the pinch of regulatory legislation in their economic and social life. But until very recently this expansion of governmental power has been regarded by the mass of our citizens as a purely temporary affliction, something that would diminish when sanity was restored to its proper place in Washington. In fact to this day one can find in the pages of such journals as *The Na-*

tional Review gleeful announcements that the state has begun to wither away, as evidenced by some isolated social phenomenon or another. It is only in the past ten years that the Republican Party has acknowledged that it cannot and will not try to eliminate governmental planning in the economic sector of our national life.

Once all truly responsible elements in our society recognize the implications of this rapid expansion of government authority at Federal, state, and local levels, the time will be ripe for a new approach to the challenge of political action. When men no longer tell themselves that the next election will reverse fifty years of history and restore private initiative to its former primacy in community planning, they will inevitably begin to look with more concern and respect at the processes by which the country's laws are administered. It is my own judgment and that of more learned observers that such a point has been reached in our history. Today all but a few extreme rightists admit the need for socialized responses to the nation's most serious problems. Men differ about the proper degree and thrust of governmental intervention, but few of them, even among conservatives, deny the validity of such programs.

Thus, the time is right for the new politics as it applies to the democratization of political parties. As the powers of government increase, the effectiveness of the mechanisms which control that power must increase also. As more people find more and more of their lives being planned by the instrumentalities of the state the number of those willing to assume their political burden will rise sharply, *if there are leaders willing to interpret the problem and give guidance to their efforts.*

The task which confronts the new politicians is a difficult one. But they have going for them a significant and often overlooked eccentricity of American political life. In the United States power within parties moves *upward* from the grass roots. In spite of all that is wrong with it, our anti-political tradition has at least this one virtue. It has kept control of national party decisions in the hands of state and local leaders. Its national councils are little more than façades and figures of great reputation on the world scene are often unable to command fifty votes at a national convention. This fact explains the Presidential nominations of both Barry Goldwater and Richard Nixon. While the Scrantons and the Rockefellers were building impressive images on nationwide television, Senator Goldwater and Attorney Richard M. Nixon were going from town to town in the South and Midwest making speeches in support of a host of local candidates for minor offices. They were tirelessly available on the "creamed chicken circuit" and would speak wherever a few party faithful gathered together. As a result Goldwater and Nixon tapped the real source of convention strength, the gratitude and support of those lesser party lights with whom the power finally rests.

The process is the same at all levels of our political life. State legislatures are loaded with men whose primary qualification for office is their success in filling some municipal post to the satisfaction of municipal leaders. And the Congress of the United States is recruited very largely from the ranks of those who have "proven" themselves in one or more subordinate positions.

We are dismayed by this process when it puts a man into some key Senate chairmanship because he was for twenty years the most popular county commissioner in his state. And this way of doing business does result in a great deal of hopeless incompetence in high places. But the opposite side of the coin is the fact that those who are committed, as are the new politicians, to working hard at the grass-roots and pavement level of politics are digging into the ground from which real power grows. The men who influence the wards and precincts are the ones who also shape the foreign policy of the nation. That realization ought to put zeal into many a discouraged doorbell-ringer!

Will the young people who have demonstrated deep concern over Viet Nam, racism, and environmental pollution while students carry on the battle with equal vigor out in the non-academic community? The answer is by no means certain. The rhetoric of revolution is heady wine and does not always travel well. Those who are willing to give their lives at the barricades sometimes offer far less at the polls. But the conjunction of youthful passion and political evolution in our time gives us some basis for optimism. The history of the past decade makes it obvious to even the most indifferent observer that politics is, indeed, the first duty of every citizen.